Learning is a
Verb

The Psychology of Teaching and Learning

SECOND EDITION

Sherrie Reynolds

TEXAS CHRISTIAN
UNIVERSITY

Holcomb Hathaway,
Publishers
Scottsdale, Arizona 85250

Library of Congress Catologing-in-Publication Data

Reynolds, Sherrie.
    Learning is a verb : the psychology of teaching and learning / Sherrie Reynolds.—2nd ed.
        p. cm.
    Includes bibliographical references and index.
    ISBN 1-890871-61-3
    1. Learning, Psychology of.   2. Teaching—Psychological aspects.   I. Title.

LB1060.R49 2005
370.15'23—dc22   2004020074

Editor: Colette Kelly
Production: Sally Scott
Composition: Aerocraft Charter Art Service
Art: Lauren Kolesar, John Wincek

Copyright © 2005, 2000 by Holcomb Hathaway, Publishers, Inc.

 Holcomb Hathaway, Publishers
6207 North Cattletrack Road, Suite 5
Scottsdale, Arizona 85250
(480) 991-7881
www.hh-pub.com

10 9 8 7 6 5 4 3 2 1

ISBN 1-890871-61-3
          978-1-890871-61-1

Printed in the United States of America.

This book is dedicated to Matthew Reynolds,
a true scholar, a delightful person, and
an incredible son.

Contents

Emotion, Relationships, and the Emergent Mind   29

Mind Over Matter   41

Learning, Remembering, and Understanding   63

The Social Aspect of Ideas   93

Learning as a Condition for Teaching   113

Epilogue   131

Preface

What has to change is our fascination with nouns, to be replaced by a fascination with process.

—ANTOL HOLT

I once asked a friend of mine who is a nun why sisters ever started wearing habits. She said that they adopted the dress of the poor people with whom they worked so that they could fit in and appear to be one of them. As time went on fashions changed, but the nuns' clothing did not. Eventually there came a time when their clothing was unique and set them apart, doing the opposite of what it was originally intended to do.

Somewhat the same thing has happened in schools. According to Yvonna Lincoln, a professor at Texas A&M University, public education was largely shaped by the Industrial Revolution and was, in part, designed to prepare farm children to work in factories. Children sat in rows and worked in time segments marked by the ringing of bells. There was an emphasis on uniformity, following directions, and respecting authority. All of these and many other less obvious aspects of schooling were designed to fit children to factory life. Most of us have never questioned whether these are good things because our ideas about schools are deeply rooted in our own school experience. When something is familiar we don't usually wonder why it is the way it is.

We are in a period of tremendous change. Most of us are aware that schooling may not be working as well as it could, even though we are unsure about what is wrong and how to fix it. Many people, in their frustration, blame the teachers, the kids, or their families.

I've heard elementary school teachers talk about how the kids don't seem to be as imaginative as they used to be and that tried-and-true lessons that used to "work" don't work any more. High school teachers complain that teenagers can't write, read, or do math the way they used to. University professors complain that students are ill prepared, they don't trust research, and they don't relate to text.

There is an overall recognition that things have changed, that students are not the same, and that the old ways do not work any more. This is not an illusion. In many ways we do not live in the same world that we once did and schools and teaching must change to accommodate this. There are ideas about teaching and learning that have not been accepted into mainstream thought completely, but that hold promise for the kind of changes that need to be made. The purpose of this book is to integrate these ideas about perception, learning, and thinking as they relate to educational settings.

Origins of This Book

For eight years I worked closely with Kathleen Martin, who is a professor of mathematics and science education. She is a remarkable teacher and has a gift of knowing how to create settings in which children can explore and learn. Our work was supported by grants from the Exxon Education Foundation and the National Science Foundation. These grants were the basis for collaboration with the Fort Worth Museum of Science and History and Lockheed-Martin Corporation to create a space in the museum that is used as a laboratory for educational projects during the school day and as an exploratory space for museum visitors the rest of the time.

I have had the opportunity to observe children in many different settings in this space for as little as a half day and as long as three weeks. We create learning environments with interesting phenomena, devices, and tasks that are intended to illuminate and further children's understanding of important ideas in mathematics and science.

I have also had opportunities, through these grants, to talk with teachers and to spend time in schools. For the most part I found teachers to be very conscientious, concerned people; very few were just putting in time and working for pay. Most of them wanted the best for their students and worked very hard to provide what they thought was the best. I also found that teachers as a group are woefully uninformed about learning. In fact, it seemed to me that the things I am most concerned with as an educational psychologist are invisible to them. It isn't that they don't care about them or don't think they are important, it is that they do not think about them at all.

I have studied several unrelated fields. It is hard to trace the effects of any one of these influences, but I remember that it all began to come together when I read Gregory Bateson's work. Bateson is one of the single most important thinkers of our age and I deeply regret that I met him only in print. He began his professional life as an anthropologist and later became interested in epistemology. One of his most powerful books is *Mind and Nature,* in which he discusses the kind of knowing that connects us with the natural world. As I read his work, I had a strange sense that what he wrote was more true than anything I had read before. It was, at the same time, so fragile that I would understand it one moment and not understand it the next. It was like a sound on a badly tuned radio where I could turn the knob and, just as it became crystal clear, I turned a bit too far and the sound was distorted again.

I have read many other books in which the authors appear to be writing from this same new place from which Bateson writes, intellectual companions who have identified a piece of the path not taken. In my work and in this book I have tried to be true to their work and to relate their ideas to the everyday experience that should be the subject matter of psychology.

A change is occurring in our time. It is an intellectual revolution of the magnitude of the change that occurred during the Enlightenment. It is a perspective that allows us to see relationships, patterns, transformations, and change. This point of view is especially hopeful for psychology and education, since their subject matter is people, and people are complex and difficult to study.

Organization of the Book

Throughout the book I have used examples from daily life whenever possible. This is partly because I think these personal narratives are most likely to be shared by people reading the book since, on some level, we are alike and tend to have similar experiences. It is also because I believe deeply that psychology should shed light on the everyday experiences of ordinary people. As Bateson (1988) says, "A story is a little knot or complex of that species of connectedness which we call relevance" (p. 13).

Teaching and learning are so deeply interwoven for me that they can't really be separated. But, for the most part, I focus more on learning in the first part of the book and treat teaching in the last chapter because teaching, as I see it, must rest on a deep understanding of the human mind.

Chapters 1 and 2 of this book provide a brief review of the major cultural shifts that have occurred and are occurring in the way we think about learning. This overview creates a context for the rest of the chapters. One of the reasons to study the history of ideas is that it helps us to understand how our own thoughts have been formed. If we don't know where a view came from, or that there have been other ways of thinking about something, it is easy to think that the current thought is some sort of final and absolute truth. Another reason for teachers to be aware of some of these historical ways of thinking about ourselves is that such ideas are taken up by our culture. They become part of our language and seep into our everyday life and folk psychology. If we are not aware of the origins of these ideas we can not make a conscious choice about their validity, and they continue to influence us without our knowledge.

Chapter 3 is about the way the brain develops. Fifty years ago we thought that brain development was largely determined by biology and mostly completed at birth. Today we know that children's experiences contribute to the continued building of their brains. We know that the brain continues to add connections and grow new neurons well beyond school age. This means that adults are responsible for helping children build capacity, not just learn content.

Chapter 4 is about our sensory connections to the world and the ways these processes form, and are formed by, thought. The work of Ulric Neisser, a psychologist, and Adelbert Ames, an ophthalmologist, is the bedrock of this chapter. These two men, more than any other, helped me to understand that seeing and hearing are not the passive reception of data that they once seemed to be. There are vast, wonderful unconscious processes of thought that are a part of the simplest act of seeing and hearing. We are capable of magnificently complex, instantaneous calculations that provide us with visions and sounds. Because we do not control these processes and are not aware of them as they occur, we think of them as being much simpler than and different from what they are. We misjudge the complexity of perception because we are aware only of the results and not the process by which the results are produced. In the same way, we misjudge learning. In Chapter 4 I introduce the notion that learning is an active mental process, a theme that will be further expanded in later chapters. Chapter 4 also discusses two fundamental ways that people orient to their environment: exploring and attending.

Chapter 5 explores the various ways we relate to knowledge and information. The first part is about using information and brief remembering, both of which are quite useful, but only marginally included as a learning process. It discusses learning by trial and error, how habits develop, and how we compress knowledge into "headlines." The last part of this chapter examines the construction of understanding and the relationship between action and understanding. This chapter is heavily influenced by Piaget's work and presents his ideas as they relate to the development of understanding and of thought processes.

Chapter 6 is about the social nature of ideas and the evolution of mind. Structures of thought develop and are transformed, both culturally and individually. The construction of understanding is a self-organizing, self-regulating social process. It is regulated by what Kauffman called "order for free," the kind of order and control that emerges rather than being imposed.

Chapter 7 suggests models of teaching for active and meaningful learning. This chapter addresses the problem of schooling, which is more complex than thinking about individual or cultural intellectual development. Schools are faced with the problem of providing information as well as cultivating understanding, and these processes must be designed in ways that can be effective for groups of children. A school is an academic community guided by the purpose of creating a bridge between culturally held and valued knowledge and the development of individual understanding, between intuitions and idiosyncratic thought and more formal, communicable expressions of it. This chapter explores some of the conditions that help to nurture children's thought, including ways to help children learn adult forms of social interaction.

Schools must change radically. As Sergiovanni and Duggan (1990) say: "We do not need to remodel the schoolhouse, we must build it anew" (p. 5). In fact, I think if we do not do so schools are going to be like the habits worn by my nun friends. Having begun as a way of preparing children for everyday life, they will, by not changing substantially, become an anachronism—a place out of time in which children study something so disconnected from everyday life as to seem like an ancient rite of passage.

Acknowledgments

I would like to thank the following individuals, who reviewed this book and offered constructive suggestions for improving it. The book is better as a result of their efforts: Kathy Cooter, Texas Christian University; Christopher Hakala, Lycoming College; Susan Hanley, University of Southern Maine; Carlette Hardin, Austin Peay State University; Kathleen Martin, University of Washington, Bothell; and Virginia Richardson, University of Michigan.

I cannot express how much the love, care, encouragement, and assistance of Diane Murray has meant in the preparation of this book. I would also like to thank June Guinan, Beverly Ross, Bill, and Dr. Bob, without whom the book would not have been written. Thank you to Kathleen Martin, my colleague for many years, whose fingerprints are on many of the thoughts expressed here. Thanks to Mary Roby, D. M. Miller, Jim Day, Bud Littlefield, and Jane Conoley, who helped me get to this point; to Jeanette Gallagher, who helped with my studies of Piaget; and to Kathy Cooter, who helped with my study of Vygotsky.

Thank you to Mary Subramaniam and Glenda Clausen, who labored to type and re-type the manuscript, track down references, and all the other things that helped the book take its final form. Thanks to Teri Lubbers, Bill Voss, Fran Huckaby, Anne Herndon, and Chip Lindsey for providing feedback on the manuscript.

I also wish to acknowledge the Exxon Education Foundation, the National Science Foundation, and Lockheed-Martin Corporation for supporting the research from which this book was begun.

Fifteenth-century Europeans "knew" that the sky was made of closed concentric crystal spheres, rotating around a central earth and carrying the stars and planets. That "knowledge" structured everything they did and thought, because it told them the truth. Then Galileo's telescope changed the truth.

—JAMES BURKE

From Harmony to "Certainty"

A Brief History of Thought About Teaching and Learning

The Pre-Modern and Modern Periods

A
s we grow older, our ideas and understanding change. The warmth and amusement we feel when we listen to the way young children think about the world is partly amusement at our former selves and acknowledgment of our own growth.

In the same way that we grow and change individually, we also grow and change culturally, as groups of people. As we come to new understandings and ways of thinking about the world, we also come to new ways of thinking about ourselves.

These shifts in thought are not "clean sweeps" and they are not necessarily permanent. Old ways of thinking are not suddenly swept away completely and replaced by new ones. When new ways of thinking begin to permeate the culture, they do not do so everywhere all at once.

A detailed description of the history of thought is not possible within this book. Rather, what I hope to do is to point to some of the important turns in the road and to reveal some of the highlights. Each of the major schools of thought has been useful or it wouldn't have been accepted for so long. At the same time, each of these points of view is limited and partial, because all human knowledge is limited and partial. We operate on the best knowledge available at any given time. Even when better ideas come along, old ideas that were useful continue to be part of our thinking. Although Einstein's theory of relativity is the current standard in physics, some calculations are still made using Newton's ideas.

Pre-Modern Thought: Balance and Harmony

T
he period from the beginning of recorded Western history until the scientific and industrial revolutions (17th and 18th centuries) is referred to as the "Pre-Modern" period (Doll, 1993, p. 19). During this time, the earth was considered the center of the universe. If you've ever been camping, sailing in rough waters, white-water rafting, or anything of that sort, you have had a glimpse into the way life might have been for people who were totally at the mercy of nature. This circumstance naturally entered into their worldview.

Having this experience of fragile humanity in the face of powerful natural forces, pre-modern people believed they had to bring themselves into harmony with nature. Much of their belief system about their world was rooted in this need to align themselves with powerful natural forces.

Early people believed that the earth was the center of the universe, covered by a canopy above which lived the gods in the heavens. These people thought that rain was caused by the ocean above the canopy leaking. They hoped that the gods could be persuaded to protect them. They were not trying to control their environment. Instead, they were trying to bring themselves into harmony with nature and the will of the gods.

The Greeks expressed this idea of harmony in their symmetrical architecture. Further, in the world of that time excess represented a lack of balance and was to be avoided. Harmony meant an emphasis on how pieces of knowledge fit together rather than an accumulation of knowledge, especially not an accumulation of one specific kind of knowledge. The focus was on unity and a sense of interconnectedness. In such a worldview, people and nature are one. This Greek ideal resides today in the notion of a "well-rounded person" and a wide-ranging liberal arts college education (Doll, 1993).

In that time, knowledge was not something to be *acquired*. Truth was eternal and unchanging, and people were assumed to always have known it. In this context, teaching was a means of helping people to remember these truths that they already knew. The *Socratic method*, set forth by the famous Greek philosopher Socrates, was intended to assist students in remembering these truths. Socrates would engage a student in dialogue and, by only asking questions, bring the student to "remember" ideas and thereby gain insights.

The experience of "remembering" or "recovering" insights may sound familiar to you. At times it may not seem that a new idea came from someplace outside of you. Instead, the idea seemed to be inside and emerged with more and more clarity during the course of the conversation.

Modernism: The Mechanical Universe

The period following the Pre-Modern era brought little change. This time has been referred to as the Dark Ages. The period from the scientific and industrial revolutions in the 17th and 18th centuries until the early to the mid-1900s is considered the "Modern" period. Most of the ideas associated with this period still form our culture and shape our lives today. Whereas the ideas associated with Pre-Modern times might seem strange and remote to most of us, the period of Modernism is so familiar that we might not have given it much thought or questioned it. We are likely to accept these ideas as truth, reality, or simply the way things are. Although these ideas are familiar and comfortable now, at some future time they will seem like ancient ideas of a people caught in a certain way of thinking during a specific period, or era, in history.

Major Thinkers of the Modernism Era

The first person to look into "the heavens" was Galileo (1564–1642), inventor of the telescope. He came to believe that the sun, not the earth, was the center of the universe. This—and the development of mathematics and science—marked a dramatic shift in the way people thought about themselves and their world. "Galileo saw mathematics as the alphabet God used in writing Nature's Laws" (Doll, 1993, p. 20).

The basic relationship between people and nature began to shift. Nature no longer was to be supplicated "through ritual and prayer" (Doll, 1993, p. 20), nor were people focused solely on working in harmony with nature. Following Galileo, the discoveries of Isaac Newton (1642–1727) gave humanity even more control over nature. "No longer was the vision one of working in moderation with Nature; it was now that of civilizing nature, improving it. Progress and perfection seemed possible, even inevitable" (Doll, 1993, p. 21).

As a result of Newton's theories, and Galileo's discoveries before him, people began to think of the universe as stable, linear, and immutable. They began to conceive of the earth as a cog in a large, machine-like universe. Like any machine, the universe was assumed to operate according to laws and principles that, if discovered, could lead to prediction and control. Natural phenomena that formerly appeared mysterious or immutable now could be understood by breaking them down into parts. By understanding the parts, people could understand the whole.

Charles Darwin (1809–1882) was another modernist thinker. His theory of evolution changed the way people perceived the relationship between people and animals. Prior to Darwin each species was assumed to be a distinct and separate entity. Darwin established continuity between animals of different species and between animals and humans. For the first time, people could study some facets of animal behavior as a means of gaining insight into human behavior, because of the new hypothesis that animals and humans are related.

The philosopher René Descartes (1596–1650) reasoned that the machine-like component of life is shared by humans and other animals but that humans have an additional quality called mind, or soul. Descartes considered the mind to be free and not bound by mechanistic laws, a qualitatively different entity. He expressed this notion in the provocative quote, "I think; therefore I am." Objective knowledge, which encompasses all but the human soul, can be studied scientifically, whereas subjective knowledge (the mind, or soul) cannot. This concept is known as *mind/body dualism*. Most of us are so accustomed to thinking of ourselves from this mind/body dualistic perspective that we might have trouble imagining anything different.

Practical Knowledge

Additional developments in modern philosophy had a profound impact on thinking about the culture in general and psychology and education in particular. According to scholars, the founders of Modernism introduced the following types of practical knowledge:

1. Questions of proof, which could be written down and analyzed, replaced questions of argumentation (rhetoric).
2. General, universal principles superseded specific cases and specific conditions.
3. The search for abstract, general ideas usurped the increasing amounts of experience by individuals and particular instances.
4. The timeless replaced the timely.

These developments were in accord with the general movement of science. Science was searching for universal principles in decontextualized environments, such as laboratories, as opposed to earlier periods when scientists tried to understand daily life in its naturally occurring contexts. For Descartes, as well as other Modern-era philosophers and scientists, "their aim was to bring to light permanent structures underlying all the changeable phenomena of Nature" (Tryphon & Vonèche, 1996, p. 37).

In this conceptualization, not all practical knowledge was included. The practical knowledge that was excluded was a mainstay of preliterate cultures: narrative stories. Though narratives have often been discounted as a legitimate component of modern practical knowledge, they still hold an important place in most of our lives, and are best known as storytelling.

Some researchers think that narratives contain important knowledge. In recent years, books have entered the market telling the stories of everyday people's experiences of historical events such as slavery. Some schools are using these "oral histories" as a way of making history come alive for their students and preserving knowledge that is about to be lost. In one high school history class, the teacher had her students interview people who lived through World War II, compile the stories into a book, and give each interviewee a copy.

Thought as Association

In the context of Modernism, knowledge no longer was considered to be inborn or something to be remembered. People who were interested in human thought and experiences began to use experiments to try to understand phenomena that could be measured scientifically. Researchers created carefully controlled laboratory settings and analyzed their experiments "to discover the basic elements of mind and the ways in which these elements combine" (Luria, 1979, p. 21). For example, a psychologist interested in the experience of feeling full after eating asked his subjects to swallow a balloon. The balloon then was inflated while the subject reported on his sensations.

These researchers looked at the mind as if it were a machine and decided that ideas are organized through associations. Ideas that occur together frequently form an association. Associations with other ideas form concepts and theories, thereby expanding and reorganizing the more primitive relationships into complex systems of relationships.

According to Luria (1979), "A basic distinction within psychology formed around the basic 'building blocks' of the mind that the psychologist assumed" (p. 8). One group, called the structuralists (Schultz, 1975), postulated that sensations combine to form simple ideas or habits that recombine to form more complex ideas. This group believed that thought could be studied in the same way as a physical phenomenon, such as the path of a falling object, and attempted to find basic laws of association that would account for the way sensations combine to form elementary ideas. This group included Wilhelm Wundt, E. B. Titchener, John Watson, and Clark Hull. Their work was published in the 1800s.

Also according to Luria (1979), another group, made up of Franz Brentano, William James, and the Gestalt psychologists, "resisted this 'elementarism'" (p. 9). These researchers believed that the mind could not be studied by analyzing its elements, because that would "obliterate properties of the intact, functioning organism that could not be retrieved once the reduction had taken place" (p. 9). They believed that when elements are brought together, something new is formed that is not in the elements, but in the whole created by them.

Also during the late 19th and early 20th centuries, psychoanalysts following the tradition begun by Freud and Jung were interested in using the idea of association to solve clinical problems through the "talking cure." They believed that during childhood we form associations that—particularly if they are traumatic—become unconscious. This unconscious material continues to control us without our awareness.

The application of *free association*, among other techniques, was designed to uncover this unconscious material through associations. For example, in a typical free association the analyst says a word and the patient is to say the first thing that comes to mind. Therefore, I might say "blue" and you say "Monday." I gradually move to words that I believe are linked more directly to your problem. So when I say "mother," your response is assumed to reveal your subconscious or unconscious thoughts.

Operationalism

In the 1920s, operationalism developed out of these early associationist ideas and came to dominate research. Operationalism is the belief that ideas or findings are dependent upon (and therefore defined by) the operations used in arriving at them. For example, "intelligence"—which is used in everyday language to refer to a variety of behaviors—became *operationally* defined as performance on an intelligence test. This definition seems to be more precise than the common uses of the word. It enabled measurement by physical, observable referents. When we speak of intelligence in everyday life, by contrast, we do not mean just that which is measured by an intelligence test, so while the operational definition appears more precise, it may be less meaningful.

In operationalist thought, all concepts that could not be measured were discarded. Thus, the study of the mind was reduced to the study of operations and physical observables. People were studied in the same way as objects, from what the biologists Maturana and Varela (1987) later call "an observer's point of view." The limitations of this view are only now becoming clear.

Modernist Learning Theory and Education

Shifts in thought about the world and its people over time created major concurrent shifts in views of teaching. Clearly, teaching is a different enterprise when it is viewed as a process of helping students remember what they already know (as in Pre-Modernism) than when it is a process of helping a student build knowledge from scratch (as in Modernism). In teaching, this means that the student is seen as a blank page on which the teacher can write the knowledge. The teacher is to *transmit* knowledge. Teaching is referred to as a delivery system. The emphasis no longer is on bringing forth knowledge *from* the student but, rather, on delivering knowledge *to* the student. In this situation, teaching focuses on the most efficient ways to "deliver" knowledge. The emphasis is on the quantity of knowledge delivered and on *teaching* rather than on *learning.*

The belief that knowledge is discovered through the senses (and tools that extend the senses, like microscopes) and elaborated through association, ultimately led to a psychological school of thought called behaviorism (discussed below), which dominated American education until recent times. The roots of behaviorism are found in classical conditioning.

Classical Conditioning

Charles Darwin established a basis for research on animals to be used as a way to understand humans. Darwin's principle of natural selection described how physical change occurred over time, generating new types of life. This idea was so powerful, and it fit so well with the tenor of the times, that natural selection was later taken up as a way of thinking about intellectual and social change. Darwin believed that natural selection leads to improvement of the species by making it better suited to the conditions of life. Clearly, an organism that can learn, think, and remember is better suited to survive than one guided completely by instinct or reflexes.

Darwin believed that nature produces an abundance from which natural selection winnows out the best. This idea found its way into behavioral psychology as the notion that organisms (animals and people) emit behaviors from which the environment selects that best suited to it. Both are adaptive processes in which an organism adapts to an environment that is making demands on it.

These two ideas, using animals to study human psychological events and learning as an adaptive process, came together in the work of Ivan Pavlov on classical conditioning. Pavlov was a Russian physiologist who won the Nobel Prize in 1904 for his study of digestion. He noticed that the dogs in his experiment salivated when the lab assistant approached with food. He saw parallels between this and the physiological events he was studying. In fact, in his acceptance speech for the Nobel Prize, he said, "In a word, the experiments with psychical stimulation prove to be exact, but miniature, models of the experiments with physiological stimulations by the same substances" (Cuny, 1965, p. 123). This was an important breakthrough, making it feasible to study psychological events through their physiological manifestations.

Pavlov created an experiment in which he allowed a dog to smell liver powder, in the presence of which the dog naturally salivates. While the dog smelled the liver powder, Pavlov rang a bell. Of course, dogs do not naturally salivate to the sound of a bell. Pavlov's question was whether the ringing of the bell would become associated with the liver powder and lead the dog to salivate when the bell sounded and the liver powder was not present. That is exactly what happened.

Pavlov's demonstration led to the notion that all learning can be explained by simple reflexes that, through association, become elaborated into more complex ideas, attitudes, and actions. This process is known as "classical conditioning." In 1913 John Watson saw the possibility to use these ideas to "develop techniques whereby he could condition and control the emotions of human subjects" (Schultz, 1975, p. 175). He began a revolution, calling for psychology (and the study of learning) to become "a totally objective psychology—a science of behavior—dealing only with observable behavioral acts that could be objectively described in terms of stimulus and response" (Schultz, p. 176).

The adoption of "objective psychology" spelled the end of introspection as a way of understanding psychological events. Psychology was to be studied using the same methods as physiology, reducing the study of interior experience to that which can be described by an outside observer. Such a reduction fit well with the values and goals of the Modern period.

Behaviorism

John Watson (1874–1949), considered the founder of behaviorism, issued a "manifesto" in 1913, in which he argued "that psychology should be defined as the study of behavior" (Skinner, 1974, p. 5). Watson was impressed by what an organism could learn to do through conditioned reflexes. He believed that these reflexes must be the basis for learning and that the study of animals could be extended to the study of humans. He acknowledged that humans are more complex than animals but felt that the basic underlying principles are the same. He believed that "all animals . . . were extremely complex machines that responded to situations according to their 'wiring', or nerve pathways that were conditioned by experience" (WGBH Interactive Media, 1998, p. 1).

The most famous behaviorist, B. F. Skinner (1974), who advanced behaviorist concepts, wrote that "the reflex suggested a push–pull type of causality not incompatible with the nineteenth-century concept of a machine" (p. 6). Behaviorism tries to understand people by describing what they *do*—their behavior. It is based on the principle that "what people have often done they are likely to do again" (Skinner, 1974, p. 13). Most of us use this idea, consciously and unconsciously, in our daily life. When I was in high school, my English teacher began a conversation by telling me that I should go to college. After she had started the conversation that way three days in a row, I came to expect the conversation to begin that way. She had operationalized the concepts of the behaviorists.

Another form of behaviorism is referred to as the "psychology of the other one" (Skinner, 1974, p. 14). This approach limits study to that which can be observed in the behavior of a person in relation to his or her prior history in that environment. Suppose, for example, a behaviorist is asked to help a teacher deal with a student who is not staying in his seat. The first step is to chart the student's behavior. She might tally the number of times the student gets up in an hour and also chart the student's other behaviors during that hour. This is done to establish a *baseline*, or record of the child's current behavior, both as a way of finding out how to change the behavior and as a way of seeing when the behavior changes. In the tradition of operationalism, Skinner (1974) said:

> Since no two observers can agree on what happens in the world of the mind, then from the point of view of physical science mental events are "unobservables"; there can be no truth by agreement, and we must abandon the examination of mental events and turn instead to how they are studied. (p. 16)

This form of behaviorism does not deal with variables such as feelings, mind, or consciousness. Behaviorism limits the study of human beings to the study of outwardly observable behavior. According to Skinner, a robot and a person, behaving in exactly the same way, are indistinguishable (p. 16).

Radical behaviorism is a form of behaviorism that does not deny the usefulness of self-observation, but it explains the apparent world of consciousness, mind, or mental life as a reflection of physical, bodily structures. Thus, the separation of mental and physical realities that dates back to the Greek philosophers culminates in the *reduction* of mind to body. Radical behaviorists explain the mind in this way: "What has evolved is an organism, part of the behavior of which has been tentatively explained by the invention of the concept of mind" (Skinner, 1974, p. 50).

Radical behaviorism holds that people can be understood, and behavior predicted, by knowledge of their genetic and environmental histories. The process by which people adapt to their environments is an extension of Pavlov's classical conditioning. In this case, consequences following actions that confer a survival advantage, such as those resulting in obtaining food, are rewarded, or reinforced, by this consequence and, thus, are more likely to recur.

The radical behaviorists called this *instrumental conditioning.* Whereas in classical conditioning the experimenter is limited to inborn reflexes such as salivation, instrumental conditioning escapes that limitation.

The basic idea is that when a reinforcer follows a paired stimulus and response, the association, or bond, between the stimulus and response is strengthened. A reinforcer is anything that increases the probability of the response occurring after a stimulus is presented.

This expansion of classical conditioning allowed behaviorists to greatly extend the range of conditioning as an explanation of learning. Any behavior that brings about a survival advantage can be considered a reinforcer. Thus, behaviorists believe, for example, that actions that result in obtaining food are reinforced when eating relieves hunger.

In child rearing, people often question whether or not to do something out of concern that "it will only reinforce that behavior." This concept is exemplified by the child who kept getting out of bed at night and coming into her parents' bed. The mother followed the advice given in child-rearing books, which suggested firmly putting the child back in bed and leaving, being careful not to "reinforce" the behavior by talking to the child. The mother followed this advice and in fact continued to follow the advice even though it was not working. The father, who had not read the book, picked up the daughter, patted her, reassured her, and put her in bed. He pulled up a chair close to the bed and, in a soft voice, told his daughter that they love her, that all family members must sleep in their own bed, and that the parents are just in the next room if she needs them. After that, the girl stayed in her own room.

As a parenting tool, reinforcement aims to control behavior without dealing with related, underlying problems. Some new parents are afraid to pick up and comfort a crying baby because they have been told it will reinforce crying behavior. Generally, when a child's need is satisfied, it does not lead to an increase in the behavior but, rather, to a sense of trust that parents will care for the child.

Behaviorism dominated the fields of psychology and education in the United States for many years. It gave rise to teaching machines, early computer-assisted instruction (CAI) programs, programs for control or cessation of unwanted behaviors, and animal training. It formed, and still forms, the basis of many classroom management programs in schools.

Scientific Management

Attempts to predict and control behavior led to the management techniques in business called *scientific management*, developed by Frederick Taylor at the Bethlehem Steel Company in 1890. Taylor said that management should specify each day what is to be done, how it is to be done, and the exact time in which it is to be done.

These ideas were incorporated into how educational curricula should be planned and used and are central to the concept of lesson planning. Doll (1993) believes scientific management has yielded some negative results:

> It assumes ends should be fixed prior to the implementation of means. Efficiency, then, is measured in terms of the number of *specific* ends achieved and the time needed for achievement. Such a linear and closed system tends to trivialize the goals of education, limiting them only to that which can be particularized. (p. 42)

Scientific management has been implicated in the concern that students often seem *technically* proficient but they do not seem to be creative or expressive in communication. "Objective" grading standards for creative writing papers, for example, include many elements of writing but lack any judgment of quality of thought or expression. Grading, and more broadly, teaching, have been transformed by scientific management principles.

According to Doll (1993), these ideas of specification and quantification became part of American culture. "Not only did American industrialism become synonymous with efficient production, but American life took on the same hue" (p. 42). Further, "scientific management" was viewed as

> *the way* to educational reform. In this move, educational reform started on a path it has remained on to the present day: defining reform in terms of "improved" management systems, not in terms of teachers' personal growth and power. (p. 42)

Technical efficiency and assembly lines, which increased productivity in factories, were adopted in schools. Multipurpose, multilevel classrooms were replaced by discrete grade levels. The school day was broken into separate time units of 35- to 40-minute segments.

Donald Schön has been critical of technical rationality. He criticized this philosophy "not only for merchandising thought—emphasizing implementation of means over choice of ends—but for negating the real world of lived practice" (quoted in Doll, 1993, p. 46).

In the age of technical rationality and behaviorism, curriculum downplays human abilities that are different in degree or quality from those of animals. Behaviorism, as the behaviorist J. B. Watson said, "recognizes no dividing line between man and brute" (Doll, 1993, p. 59). Doll says that this view has contributed strongly to a concept of curriculum wherein training in prechosen activities has superseded the development of transformative abilities—those abilities that, in Jerome Bruner's (1973) phrase allow us "to go beyond the information given" (Doll, 1993, p. 59).

Beginning in the 1950s, some educators began to recognize that the transformative abilities—purposiveness, self-organization, communication—are important and should be encouraged. These educators began to argue that, behaviorism notwithstanding, there is, in fact, a dividing line between people and brutes.

Transitions to Post-Modernism: Beginnings of the Cognitive Revolution

 hroughout the modern period, people were arguing for alternative modes of thought. Mainstream psychology, education, and culture did not welcome these new ideas, one of which was *humanistic psychology*, attributed to Abraham Maslow.

Maslow was a visionary psychologist during the period when psychology was dominated by behaviorism and Freudian psychoanalysis, the two theories that dominated thought until the 1950s. Neither perspective was satisfactory to him. He rejected behaviorism because it was inadequate to explain the complexity of human beings. And he thought psychoanalysis, based on clinical studies, did not provide a good model for understanding emotionally healthy people. World War II was in progress, and Maslow was especially concerned about what forces led people to "flock to a Hitler or a Stalin" (Hoffman, 1988, p. 150).

Maslow developed a theory of human motivation, based on human needs. He proposed the hierarchy of needs shown below. The bottom two levels of needs he called "deficiency needs" because the motivation for fulfilling them goes away once they are satisfied. The hungry person, for example, is motivated to eat, but, having eaten, the motivation disappears and other motivations replace it. The top three needs he called "being needs." When they are met the motivation does not decrease. The more one understands, the more one wishes to understand. At the top of the pyramid is self-actualization. Maslow says this is a desire to fulfill one's potential, to become everything one is capable of becoming.

Other psychologists were proposing ways of thinking about people that restored the "inner self," which had been neglected by behaviorism, as well as the study of normality, which had been neglected by Freudian analysis. These new ideas were dubbed the *cognitive revolution*—an effort to establish meaning as the central concept of psychology. Its aim was to urge psychology to join forces with its related disciplines in the humanities and the social sciences.

Bruner (1983) described the beginnings of the cognitive revolution as follows:

Take the main texts, the advanced "high status" ones. When I was a graduate student, Woodworth's *Experimental Psychology* was the book. . . . It boasts 823 pages of text. By a generous count, the topic of thinking is treated in two brief chapters, one on "Problem Solving" (including animal studies), the other on "Thinking." All told, 77 pages. When the prestigious *Handbook of Experimental Psychology* appeared in 1951, . . . , it had 1,362 pages.

Self-Actualization
Fulfillment of one's potential

Self-Esteem
Respect for self, respect of others

Love and Affection
Giving & receiving attention; feeling of belonging

Safety-Security
Ability to protect oneself from harm

Physiological Needs
Food, water, shelter, sleep, sexual expression

This time, the topic was disposed of in a chapter called "Cognitive Processes": 27 pages. . . . The mind was not doing well in psychology. The eye, ear, nose and throat fared far better: nine chapters, about 400 pages. (pp. 106–107)

In the early days of the revolution, procedural conventions were instituted to make mental processes look more "objective" (p. 107).

In 1932, one of the earliest cognitive psychologists, Edward Tolman, published *Purposive Behavior in Animals and Men*. Tolman challenged a basic tenet of behaviorism: the idea that behavior is "stamped in" by reward. Tolman argued that what gets stamped in depends upon what the animal is attending to; it is not automatic. He argued that behavior is purposeful:

You do not go around "acquiring responses." You gather knowledge and then figure out how to use it to get to your goals. Learning is not modeled on a switchboard with incoming stimuli getting connected to outgoing response. More like a maproom, knowledge comes in; it then gets organized and plotted up. It is used to guide action toward goals. (Bruner, 1983, p. 110)

Bruner and his colleagues published a book in 1956 that represented another step in the effort to elevate mental processes. Bruner, an early pioneer in the cognitive revolution, believed that psychologists should study "man as a rational being" (1983, p. 121). He quotes a review of the book:

We are concerned throughout with the discovery and creation of order in [human] cognitive life. We are dealing with a work which both studies a part of this great theme and, in itself, exemplifies it. . . . It lies in the selection, arrangement, and appropriate adequations to the objects of perception and thought, of limited traits, of a small residue of potential wealth. (p. 121)

Another emerging cognitive psychologist was George Miller. He is best known for his observation that human memory is limited to five—plus or minus two—"chunks" of information at one time. The way we expand our memory is by organizing it into larger and larger chunks. Miller says of the cognitive revolution that "even our limited victory was important, for it served to lift psychology's thirty-year ban on mentalistic terminology" (Bruner, 1983, p. 126).

The cognitive revolution, which reputedly began in the 1950s, was not immediately successful. Miller says that we had first "an oxymoron: non-mentalistic cognitive psychology" (Bruner, 1983, p. 126). The study of meaning had been subverted when the idea of *constructing* meaning was replaced early in the revolution by the idea of *processing* information (Bruner, 1990, p. 4). Psychology did not give up the idea of mind as machine. Rather it simply changed machines. The computer became the new model for the mind in a new school of psychological thought called *cognitive science.*

In 1950, A. M. Turing proposed a version of the *imitation game* to be played by a machine and a person. The imitation game was a popular parlor game of his day, in which an interrogator tried to guess the gender of a person in a closed room through his or her written responses to questions. Turing proposed that when the game is played by a machine and a person, the operational version of the question, "Can machines think?" was whether an interrogator could determine whether a machine or a person generated the responses. This came to be known as the *Turing test.*

This idea later was expressed in the notion of "computability" as the criterion of a good theoretical model. The assumption was that a theory could be written as a computer program. When the program was run, one could observe how closely it resembled the human behavior the theory describes. This would be a test of the efficacy of the theory.

Not only was the computer a means of testing theories, but it was considered a metaphor for human mind. Computers process data by representing it numerically and performing operations, which transform it. People were thought to be similar symbol-processing entities. Knowledge was redefined as information and processes performed on information.

Except for the change in metaphor, this was not a significantly different way to think about mind from the mechanistic one that it was trying to replace. It was a way to let the behaviorists back under the tent. The real cognitive revolution occurred as the result of the recovery of its original intent: the focus on construction of meaning. This has been occurring in the current era.

Summary

Pre-modern people believed themselves to be part of nature and they sought harmony with it. Their knowledge was based on an interpretation of all that happened as a result of very human-like traits of the gods. They valued harmony and balance. They cared about how knowledge fit together rather than about how much knowledge could be accumulated and, especially, about how much of one type of knowledge could be accumulated.

The modern period was known as the "mechanical universe." The invention of the machine changed life as it was known, and in the modern period the machine was the metaphor for knowledge. The work of the early scientists of the age shifted the goal from striving for harmony with nature to striving to control nature. People began to believe that through our own intelligence and reasoning, and particularly through science, people could know nature with some certainty and thus control it.

Modern ideas rooted in the thought of Darwin and Descartes, the empiricists, Associationists, and Operationalists culminated in Watson's and Skinner's behaviorist views of human behavior. Darwinism laid the groundwork by establishing continuity between animals and humans. Descartes contributed through the idea that "objective" knowledge was obtained through the study of objects from the outside. Empiricism restricted knowledge to that which can be known through the senses, and Associationism held that ideas are formed when these sensations become associated with one another.

This laid the groundwork for Pavlov's classical conditioning and, later, behaviorism's instrumental conditioning, which was viewed as a scientific, quantifiable way to study humans. Behaviorism generated a technology for dealing with people that appeared to hold the same promise as other modern technologies: prediction and control. Behaviorism became the most powerful force shaping the way we think about learning and teaching in the Modern era.

The cognitive revolution or the Post-Modern period began in this era but found more support as modern thought began to give way. The focus on constructing meaning could not really obtain a foothold until the foundational ideas surrounding it began to change. Interestingly, the same disciplines—science and math—that ushered in the Modern era spawned the new ideas that showed its limitations and began to give rise to Post-Modernism.

2

> The first method
> analyzes complex
> psychological wholes
> into *elements*. It may
> be compared to the
> chemical analysis of
> water into hydrogen
> and oxygen, neither of
> which possess the
> properties of the
> whole.
> —LEV VYGOTSKY

Post-Modernism

Order Out of Chaos

I n many ways the Modern era was about control and certainty. "Underlying this cosmological vision was a belief or faith in certainty—that certainty was attainable through 'right reason,' and that once attained, it would be lasting" (Doll, 1993, p. 59). Ongoing scientific discovery demonstrated this "lasting certainty" to be an illusion.

As we saw in Chapter 1, 20th-century schools and teaching reflected the ideas about knowledge, learning, and behavior that were dominant in the Modern era. This means that, even today, much of what we take for granted in education might be based on assumptions that no longer are supportable. To rethink teaching, we must rethink those assumptions.

The Transition

 he ideas that undermined modernist thought began in physics, where assumptions about certainty—about absolute and objective knowledge—began to unravel. The notion that science proceeds through reductionism (reducing a complex system to simpler ones) was unnecessarily limiting.

Werner Heisenberg and other quantum physicists demonstrated that certainty does not and cannot exist at the subatomic level. Albert Einstein argued that Isaac Newton did not find nature's laws written for all time, and that the world, at least the world of space and time, is better thought of in relative terms rather than absolutes. Science turned from looking at the static, unchanging aspects of the world to studying relationships and transformations. With the study of relationships and dynamic patterns beginning in physics and mathematics, this cultural revolution spread to other disciplines.

Classical science had operated by dismissing "the irregular side of nature, the discontinuous and erratic side—these have been puzzles to science, or worse, monstrosities" (Gleick, 1987, p. 3). In the 1970s, scholars in different disciplines began to find patterns in what previously had been considered disorder. These scholars joined together to find the patterns that connect; "they feel that they are turning back a trend in science toward reductionism . . . they believe they are looking for the whole" (p. 5).

The Butterfly Effect

Prediction is the great obsession of science. Scientists try to learn enough about the patterns and conditions surrounding a phenomenon to make it predictable. One of the most resistant areas in which to make predictions is one that affects us daily: weather.

When the weather forecaster says something like, "a seventy percent chance of showers," it sounds precise, and most people think it is based on a theory about weather. Most of us also are aware that these precise-sounding forecasts are often wrong. We do not understand weather, so we do the next best thing: We measure everything we can about the weather and then compare it to all the other days when the conditions were the same. Thus, if it rained 70 in 100 of those days, we come up with the 70 percent chance of rain.

This is, on a community basis, the same thing we do on an individual basis when we expect that a new experience of a phenomenon will be just like our last experience with it. Although we know that these things are not alike in all of the details, the general pattern holds, so we can make useful predictions.

Why doesn't this work for phenomena like weather? The answer, discovered by Edward Lorenz, is called the Butterfly Effect.

Lorenz's discovery was seen as the "seed for a new science" (Gleick, 1987, p. 16). He was using a computer to model weather. With his primitive computer, Lorenz had boiled weather down to the barest skeleton. Line by line, the winds and temperatures in Lorenz's printouts seemed to behave in a recognizable way. They matched his intuition about the weather, his sense that it repeated itself, displaying familiar patterns over time. But the repetitions never were quite exact. There was a pattern, with disturbances—an orderly disorder (Gleick, 1987, p. 15).

One day Lorenz wanted to examine a sequence in more detail. Instead of starting the run again, he began it in the middle by typing in the numbers straight from the printout to restart the initial conditions. Then he left the room. Upon his return, he did not find an exact duplication of the old run as he had expected. What he found was that the new run departed so far from the old one that the pattern was not recognizable after a time. It happened because, "in the computer's memory, six decimal places were stored: .506127. On the printout, to save space, just three appeared: .506. Lorenz had entered the shorter, rounded-off numbers, assuming that the difference—one part in a thousand—was inconsequential" (Gleick, 1987, p. 16).

Lorenz realized that what makes weather unpredictable is that it is a complex system, and in this kind of system, small differences lead to very large changes. This is not the way we are used to thinking about things. We think of small changes making small differences and large changes making large differences.

Now we have come to understand that this is not true of all phenomena, or even of the most interesting ones. This property is called "sensitive dependence on initial conditions," or the Butterfly Effect (Gleick, 1987, p. 23). The latter name arose because "a legendary butterfly flapping its wings in Rio changes the weather in Chicago" (Kauffman, 1995, p. 17). The idea of a Butterfly Effect is not new. It has been captured in folklore:

> For want of a nail, the shoe was lost;
> For want of a shoe, the horse was lost;
> For want of a horse, the rider was lost;
> For want of a rider, the battle was lost;
> For want of a battle, the kingdom was lost!
> (Gleick, 1987, p. 23)

If Lorenz had seen this only as bad news about weather prediction, Gleick says, Lorenz would not have planted the seed that led to the new study of complex systems. What he understood was that this unpredictability was *necessary*. He discovered that there are systems in which small scale intertwines with large scale. These systems are nonlinear, and that means "the act of playing the game has a way of changing the rules" (Gleick, 1987, p. 24). Systems of this kind could not be studied in traditional ways because they do not behave like machines.

Unpredictability is not limited to physical systems. Detailed descriptions of learning often include a sudden shift from confusion to understanding. The shift seems to be the result of a word, a phrase, an idea, or an experience—which does not seem to be substantially different from what occurred before it. From these experiences one could not figure out how to "cause" the shift. It seems random and unpredictable.

In the 1970s, a group of business people began to notice a change in the way scientists think about and do research in science. They believed this change was going to lead to substantial changes in culture, so they contracted with Stanford Research Institute to investigate the patterns of these changes and their implications for business. The result was a paper suggesting that "a fundamental shift in basic beliefs and assumptions about the nature of things and the human condition is going on" (Schwartz & Ogilvy, 1979, p. v).

Changes in Knowing

hanges in knowing are represented by changes from objectivity to perspective, from analysis of parts to study of wholes, and from mechanical models to holographic models.

From Objectivity to Perspective

The early distinction between subjective (mind, soul) and objective (objects) has begun to break down. For many years we have assumed that objective knowledge is more reliable and consistent, perhaps even somehow more true, than subjective knowledge. We are growing away from this view and beginning to understand that any view is really a perspective. We cannot escape the fact that there is an observer, and to ignore that fact creates a kind of distortion.

The physicist Heisenberg established that, even in a physics experiment, the outcome is affected by observation. This means that there is no such thing as "objective" knowledge in the sense that the term is generally used. "*Objective* connotes distance from the object of the study; subjective connotes a personal view. *Perspective* borrows from both, defining a personal view from some distance. It suggests neither the universality of objectivity nor the personal bias of subjectivity" (Schwartz & Ogilvy, 1979, p. 53). Perspective acknowledges "the role and place of the observer," but keeps "some useful distance" (p. 51).

Think about a family gathering where several of you are trying to tell a story about an event that happened years ago. If the story hasn't been told recently, likely there is bickering about the details, and each person remembers the story differently. None of you views the event or the family in the same way. Sometimes the differences are small. Sometimes they are so large that you each may sound to others like you are describing completely different families.

An important part of the quest to understand complex systems is the shift from the idea of an ultimate singular truth to be discovered by one "best" method to a "plurality of kinds of knowledge explored by a multiplicity of approaches" (Schwartz & Ogilvy, 1979, p. 52).

History has been written, until recently, from a singular point of view as if it is the story of what "really happened." In reality, it does not incorporate other perspectives. For example, accounts in school history books of World War II seldom include the experiences of women working in factories and wearing pants for the first time. The story also is told only from the perspective of the native land. U.S. textbooks, for instance, do not include a description of the same war as the Japanese saw it.

Recognizing the limitations of human life, we have begun to understand that real-life situations can be viewed in many ways. We make use of this knowledge of perspective in our everyday lives without even realizing it. We do not live, for the most part, according to what we know from science. We act as if the earth is still, for example, even though we "know" that it is spinning on its axis. Both are true in different contexts and for different purposes.

From Analysis of Parts to Study of Wholes

A complex system is one with many interdependent, interacting parts. This includes most biological systems and many dynamic physical systems. When faced with a complex system, most people today try to understand it by breaking it into smaller parts and studying the parts. This is called *reductionism*. It is partly a result of modernist ideas about the universe as mechanical and springs partly from the idea that truth can be found through analysis. Related to the shift from objective truth to perspective is the shift from the belief that truth can be found in analysis of the parts. We now know that analysis of the parts is useful in understanding the parts, but analysis of the parts does not, by itself, lead to understanding of the whole.

We are coming to understand that human knowledge is necessarily incomplete and partial. Inevitably, our knowledge of anything will have some level of ambiguity. As H. L. Mencken (1949) once said, "There is always an easy solution to every human problem—neat, plausible, and wrong" (p. 443).

From Mechanical Models to Holographic Models

We are moving from a mechanical view of the brain to a holographic one. Most of us have seen holograms—images that appear to change as we move around them. Unlike photographs, holograms appear to be three-dimensional. One of the amazing things about a hologram is that the information is distributed throughout. If you break off a piece of the hologram, you don't get a piece of the image; you get the whole image (although it is not as sharply defined). Everything is interconnected. The interconnection of knowledge means that ideas are not built up one at a time like a brick wall.

Traditional views of teaching were based on accretion—adding one brick at a time to build a "foundation" of knowledge. The mind doesn't work that way. Learning entails a kind of Butterfly Effect that gives it a dynamic, spontaneous, unpredictable character. Sometimes a passing remark or even something in an unrelated subject is what sparks a thought or an entire reorganization of thought. Jean Piaget, whose work will be examined in Chapter 5, writes about these shifts in children's thought.

We are not passive recipients of dormant facts. We are alive, and our thoughts are propelled by will, intent, and motive. We *seek* information, *make* meaning, *construct* reality. If we are seeking metaphors for learning, they must be rooted in movement, sudden connections that reorganize and make sense of things, and they must be self-directed.

Changes in Ordering

The view of order established during the Modern era was hierarchical. The assumption was that all structures are like pyramids with "an apex at which sits the 'supreme commander,' transmitting orders down through the ranks. At each level there is a similar top-down command relationship with all the lower levels" (Schwartz & Ogilvy, 1979, p. 54).

This is a consequence of the mechanical view of the universe in which anything can be seen as equal to other things on its level, as made up of parts from the level below it, or as a part in the level above it. Assuming this ordering enables us to think of change as disassembling and reassembling, or addition and deletion.

The physics of our day, especially the work of David Bohm, demonstrates a different kind of order—what Bohm calls "implicate order." Schwartz and Ogilvy (1979) cite the example of the growth of a human child:

> A child at birth is an extremely complex organism, vastly larger than the sperm and ovum present at conception. However, encoded in the invisibly small and relatively simple structure of the DNA in the two parent cells was all the information necessary to produce that very complex and relatively large organism. And making small changes at the chemical level of DNA can produce very large changes in the organism. Finally, that same information remains encoded in the DNA contained within every cell of the living and growing organism. The holographic order has this implicate-explicate quality, where information about the entire order is contained in each location within the order. (p. 54)

In this kind of order, which occurs throughout the universe, things are not connected in a line as in A → B → C. They are interconnected, like a web. Schwartz and Ogilvy (1979) use the example of a river delta with a network of streams: "It is not possible to predict the flow in any one branch of the network of streams in a delta from the flow in the mainstream of the river. The flow in any one branch depends in a complex way on flows in all the other branches" (p. 54).

When things are interconnected in that way, a change in one branch will result in adjustments in many or all of the others, but one cannot determine what will happen in any of those branches.

Thoughts are interconnected in a similar way.

Have you had the experience, about midway into the semester, of suddenly seeing a new way to think about something you've been studying? It is as if this one new idea suddenly made everything shift. When that happens, you might have to take a few days and reorganize what you know—rearrange it to reflect this new structure. This is not a linear change. It is not like pushing over the first domino in a chain of dominos. It is as if the whole thing moved *at once*. Sometimes a small addition results in a big change. Sometimes it results in a new structure.

New Models of Causality

Early thinking about causality is of "singular causes in a linear and mechanical sequence. Push the rock and it moves. Pushing it again produces the same result" (Schwartz & Ogilvy, 1979, p. 56). Newer models of causality describe more complex systems consisting of cycles involving feedback. Cause and effect, as in A → B, is replaced by the mutually causal model A ↔ B.

As an example, for many years we thought that some babies were born with a bad temperament and that this *caused* parents to react negatively. What we know now is that the more stress parents feel surrounding the birth and early life of a baby, the less they will be able to tolerate bad temperament. The stressed parents react to babies in a way that makes the baby's behavior worse, which makes the parents feel more stressed, and so on. It is a cycle of causation with no clear beginning. In this kind of system, things change together, "more or less in harmony. If the system is resilient, such a process tends to be smooth and continuous (though not necessarily slow)" (Schwartz & Ogilvy, 1979, p. 57).

Norbert Weiner's work in cybernetics in the 1940s led to alternative ways of visualizing relationships through the concept of *feedback*. Feedback occurs when information passes back to the source from which a change emanated. We use feedback when we learn to ride a bicycle. We lean, the bicycle responds; if it seems to fall too far, we lean the other way.

Without realizing it, we use feedback every time we set a thermostat in the house. Negative feedback leads to a change in direction so the system is maintained within limits. If the thermostat is set at 70 degrees for air-conditioning and the temperature in the surrounding environment exceeds 70 degrees, a switch is tripped that turns on the air conditioner. As the air cools, it falls below 70 degrees, which turns off the air conditioning. When the temperature is too high, the thermostat acts to lower it. When the temperature is too low, the thermostat acts to raise it. This illustrates the negative feedback system.

Conversely, positive feedback leads to *more* of the same direction. In the example of the thermostat, as the temperature drops, the air conditioner turns on, which causes the temperature to drop, which causes the air conditioner to turn on. This is analogous to a runaway train, what programmers call an *infinite loop*. It is the kind of feedback that makes that annoying high-pitched sound when a microphone is too close to an amplifier.

Gregory Bateson was among the first to understand people's adaptation in terms of feedback systems. His work led to thinking of families as *systems*. In the new way of thinking, psychologists, for example, began to treat children as part of a family system rather than as having a problem that resided within themselves.

In the former mechanical-universe approach the child was considered "broken," and psychologists had to find the break and repair it.

As a result of work in family systems, psychologists began to notice that as one family member was "fixed," another family member developed symptoms. They started to think of the family as a system of interrelationships. In the new model they assume that the pattern of interrelationships, rather than any one individual in the family, is what is causing the problem. If one person is having difficulty, the problem is not assumed to be in that person. Instead, the *symptoms* of a family problem have surfaced in that person.

For example, when a child or children in a family get into trouble at school, psychologists look for problems in the family, such as marital problems. In that case, the school problems temporarily unite the parents, who focus on the child, talking with teachers and the like, instead of looking toward each other. If the child's behavior improves, parents focus on the marriage again, the fighting begins again, the child gets in trouble in school, and so on. The parents do not *want* the child to be in trouble, and the child is not intentionally getting in trouble to stop the parents from fighting. Because of the complex interrelationships in families, though, that is how it plays out. Contemporary psychologists treat the family as disordered, with one or more members carrying the symptoms at a particular time.

Thus, a new way of dealing with children in classrooms developed. We have moved from thinking of children as "disturbed" (broken, in need of repair) to thinking of them as "disturbing." The problem is conceptualized as a disturbance in a system of relationships rather than a malfunction in the child. Take the case, for example, of a child who makes a remark that annoys the teacher. The teacher confronts the child and gives him or her an ultimatum. The child responds to the ultimatum by becoming more belligerent. From a behaviorist's perspective, the solution is to control the child's behavior. From a systems perspective, the problem is to stop the cycle of positive (linear) feedback.

Feedback is involved because people are interrelated. We do not act independently but, rather, in relationship with others. In modern thought, only the simplest kind of linear relationships was conceptualized. Post-modern thought has recognized and found ways to conceptualize complex systems—patterns of interrelationships and interdependencies. To understand complex systems, such as families and classrooms, we must understand relationships.

Shift to a Focus on Relationships

Gregory Bateson has written about the need to change the focus on *things* to a focus on *relationships.*

Look at your hand with the fingers extended. Most people see four fingers because they focus on the static, unchanging aspect of the hand. No matter how you move your fingers, they still look the same. Another way to look at your hand is to notice the three angles between the fingers. Move your fingers and observe how the movement changes the angles. In this view, you focus on the changing relationships between the fingers (Bateson, 1991).

The mathematician Antol Holt says he is going to have a bumper sticker made for his car saying "Help stamp out nouns." He believes we need to shift our focus from nouns to processes and relationships (Bateson, 1991, p. 63). During the 17th and 18th centuries, a time of scientific achievement, we began to focus exclusively on "things." Science advanced by concentrating on the static, unchanging aspects of the world. The Newtonian science of that time neglected change and relationship, emphasizing instead that which could be described, classified, and used in making predictions.

Teaching Does Not Cause Learning

In spite of these changes, many people still think of schooling from a modernist view. We speak as if teaching *causes* learning in the same sense that striking a billiard ball with a pool cue causes it to move. The physical metaphors that we have adopted for thinking about these processes are inadequate. We have thought of the vibrant, organic, creative processes of mind as if they were physical objects. But learning, thinking, and understanding are alive, dynamic, organic processes that can be nurtured and cultivated, but not controlled, measured, forced, or caused.

We saw in Chapter 1 that the worldview progressed through the modern, reductionist, mechanical universe to the edge of the cognitive revolution. The difference between that view of teaching and learning and the new, organic one is representative of the difference between modern and post-modern thought. The cognitive revolution has become a significant force in psychology as psychologists are constructing new ways of thinking about human thought.

Ulric Neisser (1976) and others studied the basic interface between our senses and our world. Jean Piaget and Barbel Inhelder studied the development of thought over a period of about 60 years, resulting in hundreds of publications. Lev Vygotsky (1978, 1986; Marti, 1996), Jerome Bruner (1973, 1990), and others studied the way by which language and culture mediate thought. Although the work of these scholars is different in many ways, they hold in common at least three ideas that set them apart from their Modern predecessors:

1. They reject empiricism (the belief that thought is a copy of reality) and innatism (the concept that ideas are inborn).
2. They do not believe that thought is built from simple association in a passive process.
3. They believe that meaning is important and, therefore, context and engagement are important.

We will be taking a closer look at the ideas of Neisser, Piaget, Vygotsky, and Bruner in the later chapters of the book.

Summary

Post-modern thought has emerged as a new way of looking at the world. The telescope extended our world to see at great distances, and the microscope extended our vision to the very small. Today we have found a new pair of glasses that permits us to see in profound new ways. With these post-modern glasses, phenomena that are more unpredictable and chaotic have revealed a new kind of order. Unlike previous ages, we recognize this profound shift in thought *as it is occurring.* In the chapters that follow, we will examine some new ways of thinking about processes related to teaching and learning.

The human brain is a most
unusual instrument of elegant
and as yet unknown capacity.

—STUART SEATON

3

Emotion, Relationships, and the Emergent Mind

T he Surgeon General's Conference on Children's Mental Health: Developing a National Action Agenda was held in Washington, D.C., on September 18–19, 2000. This conference, along with its companion conference, Psychopharmacology for Young Children: Clinical Needs and Research Opportunities, came into being because "the burden of suffering experienced by children with mental health needs has created a health crisis in this country" (p. 1). The major product of this conference was the *Report of the Surgeon General's Conference on Children's Mental Health: A National Action Agenda* (U.S. Public Health Service, 2000), which contains surveys of the existing situation and a blueprint for corrective action. Dr. Dan Offord, one of the conference participants, said:

> The burden of suffering of children with mental disorders is significant. In the United States, between the ages of 1 and 19, the group of conditions that lowers quality of life and reduces life chances the most are emotional and behavioral problems and associated impairments. No other set of conditions is close in the magnitude of its deleterious effects on children and youth in this age group. Children with these disorders are at much increased risk for dropping out of school, and of not being fully functional members of society in adulthood. This burden of disease includes the prevalence of mental illness, morbidity, and cost. All sectors of society are involved. . . . Furthermore, child mental disorders persist into adulthood. . . . The cost to society is high in human and fiscal terms.
>
> These are not just problems associated with youth or lack of information or even problems of behavior. These are problems that reflect serious changes in children's mental health. Fifty years ago we thought that brain development was largely determined by biology and mostly completed at birth. We believed that our task as adults who care for children was to provide basic conditions for their continued physical growth and to fill their brains with appropriate content. The inadequacy of this idea is clear when we consider how much content changes over the course of our students' lifetimes. How much of what was considered "fact" when you were born is still considered fact today? (p. 17)

Fifty years ago we did not know that the child's experiences continue to build capacity; that children are, quite literally, building a brain. We now know that the brain continues to add connections and to grow new neurons well beyond school age. This "plasticity," as neurologists call it, allows us to continue to build capacity throughout our lifetime.

Fifty years ago we thought that emotion was a base leftover of our animal natures at worse and a distraction from learning at best. Today we know that emotion is an important part of thinking. In fact, thinking and emotion cannot be separated. Thinking and emotion together help us to understand and make decisions. We now understand that the brain develops in and because of relationships. We are social beings. One of the reasons for our success as a species is that we have learned to pool knowledge. The ability to do so is built into the system.

In this chapter, I will present to you (in a very simplified form) some of the work that illustrates how the brain develops with respect to building capacity. Then I will discuss the contribution to the emergent mind that is made by emotion and relationships.

The Emergent Mind

Daniel Siegel, M.D., is a psychiatrist who has written extensively on the development of the mind. Siegel believes that the mind develops in the interaction between neurophysiological processes and interpersonal experiences. The brain not only develops socially, but, he argues, it does so by design. He summons evidence from a number of different sciences to support his belief.

To fully appreciate Siegel's argument, we need to understand how the brain functions, in a simple way. At the lowest functional level, the brain is made of neurons. (There are other elements, but in our simplified version we are going to consider only neurons.) The brain continues to grow after birth. "Most of the postnatal growth occurs within the first 3 or 4 years after birth . . . , but changes in myelination . . . and in other measures (e.g., cortical surface areas, numbers of glial cells, etc.) continued to be apparent even 70 to 80 years after birth" (Nowakowski, 1987). The cells that become neurons are produced in one part of the brain and then some of them migrate to other locations.

Neurons may interconnect with many other neurons, producing an incredible level of complexity and a certain amount of redundancy. Siegel (1999) says, "the brain has an estimated one hundred billion neurons, which are collectively over two million miles long. Each neuron has an average of ten thousand connections that directly link itself to other neurons. Thus there are thought to be about one million billion of these connections, making it 'the most complex structure, natural or artificial, on earth'" (p. 13).

No agreement exists as to precisely how experience contributes to the process of neuron death and connection, but there is agreement that it does contribute. In a simple sense, we can think of it this way: a neuron factory produces an abundance of neurons. The neurons migrate and send out an abundance of connections. Those that do not find a target or targets die. Experience strengthens the connections between neurons. The connections that grow strong tend to survive, while the weaker connections tend to dissipate.

It is not just the number of connections that determines the brain structure, it is the patterns of the connections (Greenough, Black, & Wallace, 1987). In other words, using the brain is not enough, it is how we use it that makes a difference. Greenough and colleagues suggest that

> the offsetting advantage appears to be that sensory systems can develop much greater performance capabilities by taking advantage of experiences that can be expected to be available in the environment of all young animals. Thus many species seem to have evolved such that the genes need only roughly outline the pattern of neural connectivity in a sensory system, leaving the more specific details to be determined through the organism's interactions with its environment. (p. 543)

So, even with this simple explanation, we can see that experience is more powerful than we once thought. When we create contexts for children—when we choose how we will teach, what books we will read, and where children will go—we are determining our contribution to building a child's brain. It is critical that we carefully consider how we design experiences for and with children. If a child is to develop the capacity to organize information into useful forms, for example, then we need to create opportunities for them to do it, not just see the results of someone else doing it. The story of how the periodic table (in chemistry) was developed is far more interesting than the dead results of such development. In fact, the important thing may be the ability to think about the table and re-create the process that led to its development in the first place. Similarly, for younger children, finding plant leaves and thinking about ways to describe and group them before they see how others have done it may be important. The brain, like muscle, develops that which is used; that which is not used atrophies. This is a very serious matter. When we change educational policy and experiences, we run the risk of creating a different kind of human mind.

Emotion

 ntonio Damasio begins his book *Descartes' Error* (1994) with the story of Phineas P. Gage. Gage's story is well known to students of psychology because he was the victim of a freak accident.

Psychologists often try to learn what we can from such accidents, to capitalize on what is sometimes referred to as "nature's experiments."

Gage was a railroad worker who was commended by his bosses and well liked by fellow workers and people in the community who knew him. Damasio describes the accident like this: "It is four-thirty on this hot afternoon. Gage has just put powder and a fuse in a hole and told the man who is helping him to cover it with sand. Someone calls from behind, and Gage looks away, over his right shoulder, for only an instant. Distracted, and before his man has poured the sand in, Gage begins tamping the powder directly with the iron bar. In no time he strikes fire in the rock, and the charge blows upward in his face." The iron rod, three feet, seven inches long, "enters Gage's left cheek, pierces the base of the skull, traverses the front of his brain, and exits at high speed through the top of his head" (Damasio, 1994, p. 4).

The amazing thing is that Gage was not killed. In fact, an hour after the accident, when the doctor arrived, he found Gage sitting in a chair. Gage was able to speak to the doctor on the scene and tell him what happened. Thankfully for psychology, Dr. Harlow, Gage's physician, became fascinated by this case and followed Gage closely for many years. Gage recovered from his physical injuries, had no apparent cognitive deficits, and was pronounced cured in less than two months. "Gage could touch, hear, and see, and was not paralyzed of limb or tongue. He had lost vision in his left eye, but his vision was perfect in the right. He walked firmly, used his hands with dexterity, and had no noticeable difficulty with speech or language" (p. 8). However, Damasio says, "Gage was no longer Gage" (p. 8). The change was so great that his friends felt that they no longer knew him and his employer found that he could not continue to keep him on his job. "The problem was not lack of physical ability or skill; it was his new character" (p. 8).

Damasio (1994, 1999, 2003) told the story of Phineas Gage because, in his practice as a neurologist, he has seen similar cases and these cases have led him to rethink the role of emotion in cognition. In the past, emotion has been neglected in studies of cognition. Emotion has long been associated with "base" or "animal" behavior or with loss of control. A false dichotomy has been erected as if one can approach a problem or an event either emotionally or intellectually, but not both. Damasio shows that emotion and cognition are intertwined. Modern cognitive scientists do not agree on the mechanisms or exactly how the process works, but we know that no one can, or should, be perfectly rational.

In his practice, Damasio (1999) has seen totally rational people. They are that way because they have suffered an injury to the part of the brain that experiences emotion. He described patients who could analyze choices but never decide. They were not impaired in any way except emotionally.

Damasio (2003) suggests that "emotions are built from simple reactions that easily promote the survival of an organism and thus could easily prevail in evolution" (p. 30). He says that emotion is our connection between an emotionally competent stimulus and a reaction. In the presence of an emotionally competent stimulus, he notes, the first thing that happens is appraisal. Appraisal produces a sense that the stimulus is meaningful, good, dangerous, and so forth. Appraisal determines whether we pay attention to the stimulus and, to some extent, how we deal with it. This initial appraisal is handled by the emotions. Emotions are a powerful aspect of cognition that, until now, has been largely ignored. This is why, Damasio suggests, people with damaged emotional systems but no damage to cognitive areas are not able to make decisions. They become paralyzed in the face of an overwhelming number of choices with no means of deciding among them.

On the other hand, Damasio (2003) also treated a patient he called David, who "has one of the most severe defects in learning and memory ever recorded" (p. 43). He cannot learn any new facts at all. He can't learn to recognize new people, places, or things. He treats each encounter with a person as if it is the first. Damasio's staff created situations in which they engaged David in either very positive and rewarding ways, neutrally, or in negative ways. David, of course, had no memory of any of these encounters and could not tell the experimenter anything about the staff members when he was shown photos that included the faces of those he had met in these interactions. When he was asked whom he would go to for help, however, he chose the positive individual "over 80% of the time, indicating that his choice was clearly not random" (p. 45). David was able to make decisions when his emotional system was intact even though he suffered such severe cognitive deficits.

In schools we find that reason and emotion have been almost opposed to one another. One of the ways in which education has been impoverished recently is that we have attempted to remove emotion in the misguided belief that it interferes with learning. In fact, emotion is one important factor in learning. We learn more easily that which is meaningful, that about which we are curious, that about which we care. On the first night of a counseling theories class, I asked students to search the Internet for information about psychoanalysis. The assignment was to follow any thread that interested them. It took a while to convince them that there was no "answer," no "right thing" that they were supposed to find. When they came to the next class, they were excited and alive with what they had learned. They were anxious to share their "treasures" with us. When I asked them to write that evening about how they were experiencing the class, several of them commented on this experience. They said that because they were free to follow their interest, they spent a lot more time on the assignment and read and learned a lot more than they usually did for a reading assignment. Furthermore, what I saw was that when I looked at the whole picture, at the end of the class, everything that I would have wanted them to find had been found and shared by someone. No one person had found it all, but each had found some of it and shared it with an infectious enthusiasm.

I recently taught a seminar to faculty about university teaching. I described some of the current research about how people learn. One of the faculty members in attendance later said that he realized that he learns in the way we discussed, but he doesn't teach as if he thinks the students learn that way. I think it is vital that we imagine how we learn and let that, at least in part, decide how we teach. We must, most of all, rid ourselves of the belief that learning is not supposed to be fun. Watch a baby. Babies are learning machines. They dedicate their lives to learning and they enjoy it immensely. That is how we all once were. That is how we can be again.

Nel Noddings is one of the preeminent philosophers of education in the United States. In her new book, *Happiness and Education* (2003), she wrote:

> Through more than five decades of teaching and mothering, I have noticed also that children (and adults, too) learn best when they are happy. This is not to say that harsh methods are never effective in producing rote learning, nor does it mean that intermittent vexation and occasional failure are absent from a happy student life. On the contrary, challenge and struggle are part of the quest for knowledge and competence. However, struggle is an inevitable aspect of learning; we educators do not have to invent struggles for our students, and students who are generally happy with their studies are better able to bring meaning to difficult periods and get through them with some satisfaction. (p. 2)

It is important to pay attention to children's emotions and, especially, not to try to talk them out of having them. It is important to honor students' emotions so that they can learn to make better use of them. That does not mean that they have a license to act on them. One of the important skills we all learn is how to use emotional information appropriately. My point is that we do not have to, and should not try to, change the way students feel, but instead should help them understand what the feeling contributes and how to appropriately deal with it.

Learning is fun. We are made for it. It saddens me to walk by a classroom and not hear the sounds of learning or to look in and not see the sights of thinking. In our well-intentioned efforts to control behavior, we sometimes violate the conditions necessary for learning to occur. Learning is emotional. In the excitement and passion of discovering something new or figuring something out, we sometimes annoy others. That is also part of life. One of the differences between children and adults is that children are newer to life than we are. When we are new at something, we are sometimes carried away by emotion and tend to make a lot of mistakes. That is one of the ways we become experts. We make mistakes and learn from them, and gradually we make fewer mistakes. It is our responsibility as adults to help children learn from mistakes, not to save them from making mistakes, unless the consequences are too severe (like injury or death).

Relationships: Classic Studies

S ome of the earliest studies of the effects of mother-child relationships were conducted by Harry Harlow and his associates at the Primate Laboratory of the University of Wisconsin over a 3-year period (Harlow, 1958). In the early experiments, baby monkeys were separated from their mothers and bottle fed. These babies were healthier and heavier than the mother-raised infants, and they had a lower infant mortality rate, thus demonstrating that the nutrition supplied to the bottle-fed babies compared favorably to mother's milk.

During that study, Harlow says, the staff noticed that the baby monkeys seemed to be quite attached to the folded cloth diapers that were used to cover the bottom of their cages. They also noticed that the monkeys whose cage bottoms were not so covered did not do as well. In the next experiment, they created two surrogate, inanimate "mothers." One had exposed wire, and the other had wire mesh covered with terry cloth and features more like an adult monkey; the second monkey also had a lightbulb behind it that radiated heat. They were alike in every other way. Each had only one "breast." The infants received all of their milk through their surrogate cloth and wire mothers, although both types of mothers were in all cages. The experimenters recorded time spent with each mother and measured nutrition, growth, and so on. They discovered that even when the monkeys received milk from the wire mother, they spent most of their time with the cloth mother. This preference was exacerbated when the monkeys were afraid. The monkeys used the cloth mother as a "source of security, a base of operations" (p. 13). They would explore and investigate, periodically returning to this mother. When the cloth mother was removed from the cage, the monkeys behaved quite differently. "Frequently they would freeze in a crouched position. . . .

Emotionality indices such as vocalization, crouching, rocking, and sucking increased sharply. . . . Total emotionality score was cut in half when the mother was present" (p. 13).

Harlow says, "We were not surprised to discover that contact comfort was an important basic affectational or love variable, but we did not expect it to overshadow so completely the variable of nursing; indeed, the disparity is so great as to suggest that the primary function of nursing as an affectational variable is that of ensuring frequent and intimate body contact of the infant with the mother" (pp. 5–6).

Even though the monkeys received adequate nutrition from the surrogate mothers, and found some comfort from the cloth mother, it was not an acceptable substitute for live monkeys. According to a 1999 Whyfiles paper (http://whyfiles.org/087mother/4.html) on neuroscientist Mary Carlson, "if Harlow's monkey experiments might be considered cruel today, what can we say about the human deprivation 'experiment' in Romanian orphanages?" (p. 4). When long-time communist dictator Nicolae Ceausescu was executed in a coup in 1989,

> the orphanages were opened to a world that saw Dickensian warehouses for the unwanted. [The children had been crowded together with little adult attention or care.] Scientific study confirmed what the eye could see: The children were in the 3rd to 10th percentile for physical growth, and "grossly delayed" in motor and mental development. . . . They rocked and grasped themselves like Harlow's monkeys, and grew up with weird social values and behavior.

Even under less extreme conditions, children show the effects of early relationships. Psychologists who study these early relationships write about a phenomenon called "attachment," a term coined by John Bowlby. Bowlby (1982) says,

> No variables have more far-reaching effects on personality development than a child's experiences within the family. Starting during his first months in his relation to both parents, he builds up working models of how attachment figures are likely to behave towards him in any of a variety of situations, and on all those models are based all his expectations, and therefore all his plans, for the rest of his life. (p. 369)

Bowlby's student, Mary Ainsworth, developed a laboratory procedure to observe and rate these early attachment relationships. She calls the procedure the "strange situation" (Ainsworth, Blehar, Waters, & Wall, 1978; Connell & Goldsmith, 1982). Ainsworth's strange situation task is similar to Harlow's experiment. In the strange situation, an infant and his or her mother are brought into a room. After a period of playing, a stranger enters and sits down. After a short time, the mother and stranger begin to talk. Then the mother leaves the room, leaving the baby with the stranger. After another period, the mother returns to the room. The mother-baby attachment is rated according to how the baby reacts to the fearful situation and whether the baby seeks comfort from the mother.

Relationships: Recent Studies

Fraley (2002) reports that "most children (i.e., about 60%) behave in the way implied by Bowlby's 'normative' theory. They become upset when the parent leaves the room, but when he or she returns, they actively seek the parent and are easily comforted by him or her" (p. 2). If you are a parent, you may have left your child with a stranger; if you have been a babysitter, you may have been the stranger with whom the child was left. The way infants react in the strange situation is about what we would expect from our own experiences. Children who behave in this normative way are called "secure."

About 20 percent or fewer of infants do not react this way, however. They are

> ill-at-ease initially, and, upon separation, become extremely distressed. Importantly, when reunited with their parents, these children have a difficult time being soothed, and often exhibit conflicting behaviors that suggest they want to be comforted, but that they also want to "punish" the parent for leaving. These children are called anxious-resistant. (Fraley, 2002, p. 2)

Another 20 percent of children, according to Fraley, exhibit behaviors that were classified as "avoidant." Fraley says that "avoidant children . . . don't appear too distressed by the separation, and, upon reunion, actively avoid seeking contact with their parent, sometimes turning their attention to play objects on the laboratory floor" (p. 2). Ainsworth demonstrated that the way a child reacts to the strange situation is correlated with the way the child was parented. Children who are secure in the strange situation tend to have parents who observe and respond to their needs.

Subsequent research has demonstrated strong relationships between these early experiences and later ability to care for children and for romantic partners (Cassidy, 2001; Feeney, 1999). Poor attachment has been correlated with severe emotional disturbance (Goodman, 1998), poor social functioning, and aggression (Drotar, 2002), to name a few.

Shelley Taylor wrote an important book called *The Tending Instinct* (2002). She says that "it was a tantalizing surprise to see how clearly social relationships forge our underlying biology, even at the level of gene expression" (p. 2). She argues that one of the reasons for our success as a species is that we are social by nature. The need to tend to one another, she says, is built into our neurocircuits as surely as any other instinct, and it has contributed as much to our survival. As a social animal, our survival depended on our ability to form groups that could work closely together. To form such groups, we had to tend to one another and develop relationships. The reason we have neglected these aspects of life, she says, is that so much of our science has been done by and with males.

We believed for a long time that the human response to stress was "fight or flight." Taylor found that this is a male response to stress, rather than a human response.

When Taylor and others began to study females, they found a very different response to stress, which Taylor called "tend and befriend." They discovered that women turn to others in times of stress. Women, who tend to children, seek out other women; this, Taylor maintains, is important in our evolutionary history. If all humans fled or fought aggressors, children would have been left alone, defenseless, and vulnerable to the attack. The species likely would have died out in a few generations. Tending and befriending is not a luxury, it is vital to our existence. Things that are vital to our existence become an important part of the system and usually have redundancies built in. This means that if something goes wrong with one aspect of the system, others will make sure the activity occurs. This is what Taylor found with tending. There is a biological basis that ensures that women will perform these functions.

When children were asked what their fathers do when they've had a hard day, the children reported that fathers go in the bedroom and tell the children not to bother them. When asked the same question about their mothers, the children reported that their mothers play with and cuddle them. We respond to stress differently. Similarly, when women are stressed, they discuss their problems with friends. Men reported that, under similar circumstances, they discuss their problems with their wives.

My point in including these ideas is not to argue about differences between men and women but to suggest, as Taylor does, that we have been impoverished and misled by the exclusive focus on men's experiences. Furthermore, we have neglected an aspect of human life that is essential for brain development. Taylor's voice adds to that of Nel Noddings (1992), who has argued for years that schools should focus on teaching children to care. Now these bodies of literature are converging and demonstrating that caring for children and teaching children to care for each other and the world around them are not just nice ideas. They are imperatives for the good of our species. We know that the "genome is like an architect's first plan, a rough projection of how a person may turn out. But like most efforts, this plan is revised during the course of the building process" (Taylor, 2002, p. 5). The conditions for optimal building of a brain are those that Noddings called "caring" and that Taylor called "tending."

The good news is that studies of "earned attachment" indicate that the effects of poor parenting can be overcome with later treatment and intervention. "Resiliency" literature indicates that these interventions can be in the form of a single individual who takes interest in a child. One of the ways that we can build a brain is by building understanding relationships with children. That is not therapy, it is good teaching. Students in early grades are in a relationship with a single teacher for a significant portion of their day. We have an opportunity to impact their lives, for good or for ill.

Responding to a child, caring for a child, and tending to a child all are also synonyms for good teaching. Responding does not mean catering to a child. It means acknowledging what the child is experiencing and valuing it. It means creating conditions in which all children in our care feel understood and are thus able to grow in understanding others. This is the kind of teaching that can change a community.

Summary

Much has changed in our understanding of the brain over the past few decades. Educational practices, for the most part, were developed at a time when it was assumed that the brain is developed mostly by school age. Furthermore, many of these practices were built with faulty assumptions about the contribution of relationships and emotion to learning.

Today we know that the brain continues to build capacity throughout one's lifetime and that it is directly influenced by one's experiences. We also know that relationships and emotions are critical contributors to learning. Educators today cannot assume that learning is a matter of mere acquisition of knowledge and skills. We have an opportunity to help build a brain, and that is an awesome contribution to make to the life of a child.

With every act of
perception we
participate unawares
in making a
meaningful world.

—ARTHUR ZAJONC

Mind Over Matter

T hinking and learning arise from our most basic connection to the world around us, which is through our senses. When infants encounter a new toy, they examine it, turn it over, feel it, put it in their mouths. In more sophisticated ways, we do the same thing. Our knowledge begins in this very sensory way, both as individuals and as a culture.

Perceiving Is a Way of Thinking

W e tend to think of our senses as if they are a direct conduit bringing us pictures and sounds from the world "out there" and things "as they are." That is a useful point of view for many purposes. This idea stems, in part, from the way sensation and perception were studied traditionally.

> Most theories of perception have been constructed with vision in mind. Moreover, their model has not been the active looking of everyday life, but rather the restricted gaze of a subject who holds his head and eyes as still as possible or else is presented with a flash of illumination so brief that he has no time to move them. (Neisser, 1976, p. 15)

More recent beliefs view our sensory processes as much more beautiful, awesome, and sophisticated than the simple idea of a conduit. Without our awareness or control, our mind performs millions of complex comparisons and calculations to create the images and other sensations that make up the world as we see it. Although understanding and appreciating these unconscious processes will not allow us to control them, we might change the way in which we nurture their development in ourselves, our students, and our families.

Until the 1960s, most people thought that, in the process of seeing, a pattern of light reflected from an object onto the retina creates a direct representation of the object in the optic nerve. Maturana, Lettvin, McCulloch, and Pitts (1960) challenged this traditional view. Their study, along with Maturana and Frenk's (1963) study of pigeon vision, demonstrated that the retina does not simply pass along points of light intensity. It "performs several complex analytical operations on the visual image and it transmits to the brain a highly selected and transformed representation" (1960, p. 160).

Maturana and colleagues found that they could create a better explanation of the experience of seeing when they viewed the nervous system as a *generator* of experience rather than a *receiver* of experience. Even at the level of the nervous system, we are not passive receivers of information that the world around us forces upon us.

Warren McCulloch discovered that frogs can see a moving object that appears only at a certain angle with respect to its eye. "All else was invisible and produced no impulses on the optic nerve" (Bateson, 1991, p. 216). No matter how many insects are actually out there, they do not exist for the frog if they are not in that specific relationship to the frog's eye.

Like the frog, we have no idea whether more is out there than what we can see. We are limited. We have no idea what is really out there, because all we can know about is what we are able to detect. To poorly paraphrase Shakespeare—the limits are not just in the stars, but in our own eyes.

Extending Perception

 e have created ingenious tools that allow us to extend our senses beyond the normal ranges. Each of these tools has expanded our universe, showing us worlds that we could not have imagined previously.

Before the advent of the telescope, people believed the sky was like a big canopy with stars in it. Above the canopy was an ocean, and occasionally the ocean leaked through holes in the canopy, falling in what we call rain. The heavens, and God or Gods, were above the canopy controlling this activity. Imagine the world that opened up when our ancestors first had a tool, the telescope, to extend eyesight into the heavens! For the first time they saw not a world covered by a canopy but, instead, infinite space and other planets.

In recent years the computer similarly has opened up a new world for us. It allowed us to develop a new kind of geometry, known as "fractal geometry." This geometry has been used to create lifelike images of natural landscapes. Euclidean geometry is like looking at an object "only on a scale of an observer one kilometer away" (Gleick, 1987, p. 105). Fractal geometry is like being able to look at it from any distance. For the first time, with the advent of the computer, mathematicians could do some of their work experimentally. They could observe the results of a mathematical theory before they had mathematical proof of it. Many other disciplines have taken similar leaps.

The awesome discovery of these new worlds is reenacted each time a child looks through a microscope for the first time. What to the naked eye appeared to be a single drop of water now looks like a community alive with activity. This experience is not a new way of knowing, but it has created a new way of looking at things.

Amazing as these advances are, they still have only extended our existing senses. Our tools have given us the ability to detect the presence of objects farther away than we normally can see, to detect fainter noises than we normally can hear. Although this can be helpful, it isn't more "real" or "true." It is just different. Our senses, extended or not, connect us and our world.

The Relation Between Sensation and Thought

Ideas about the relationship between our senses and thought have shifted through the centuries. In writing about the history of science, the physicist Arthur Zajonc (1993) says, "In the Bhagavad-Gita, in Homer, Empedocles, and Plato, vision entails an essential human activity of movement out from the eye into the world" (p. 23). He notes that contemporary ideas about vision have completely reversed the process. Instead of movement *out* from the eye *to* the world, the eye is thought of as a passive recipient of images *from* the world.

People often speak of the eye as if it were a kind of camera, as if an "inner person" within the head looks at the image the eye produces (Neisser, 1976, p. 15). We now know that vision is a much more complex process, and largely a process of the mind.

Adelbert Ames Jr. (1951), an ophthalmologist, studied vision from the perspective of people's conceptions of optical illusions. Like Neisser, he found that vision is a product of the mind as much as the eye. We see as a result of the coordination of multiple inputs described in complex mathematical terms. The process is not controlled consciously, and most of us are unaware that it is happening. We deal with the coordination of all of our senses regularly and unconsciously, and we do this while moving through time and space. We regularly watch moving objects without confusing the object with the background against which it is moving. We unconsciously pick up and use information about the parts of the background that the moving object obscures and we compare these data across time to construct images of movement (Neisser, 1976).

We make comparisons over time and space to create a connected sense of an event. These comparisons are not just comparisons of sensory input; they represent organization of the input in terms of meaningful sequences. Neisser (1976) described an experiment by Gunnar Johansson, who filmed people walking in a dark room with light bulbs attached to their ankles, knees, shoulders, wrists, and elbows. "A single frame of the film shows only a meaningless pattern of dots. When the full movie is shown, however, everyone sees people walking" (p. 39). The sensory input consists of points of light that become meaningful as a result of organizing them into a familiar and useful pattern. This ability to make meaning is at the heart of thinking. It is one of the most deeply satisfying things we can do.

The mind even supplies color from the light waves the eye picks up. Color is not *in* the objects, passively received by the eye. It is constructed by the mind from the information the eye picks up and a small part of the brain processes.

Noted neurologist Oliver Sacks (1996) writes about Mr. I, an artist who lost the ability to see color as a result of a head injury. The injury was to a small area of cells on either side of the brain, about the size of a kidney bean. This area receives wavelengths of light and creates the experience of color. We do not see with the eye alone but, rather, with the eye and the mind.

Constructing Perceptions from Our Senses

Perception is not an event. Most of the time our perceptions occur continuously over time and make use of several senses. When we hear a footstep behind us, we turn around, expecting to see a person. When we see something in the distance, we continue to watch, and we might squint or shade our eyes in an attempt to see more clearly. This way of picking up perceptual information is what the psychologist Ulric Neisser (1976) called a *perceptual cycle.* When we perceive a sight, sound, touch, or smell, we orient to it and seek more information in a continuous loop of anticipation, information gathering, and modification. The process is not conscious, and it happens so quickly that we often are not aware of it.

Although Neisser and others can make us aware of how we construct perceptions, we still cannot participate consciously in the process. If we could, our participation probably would be disastrous. As Bateson and Bateson (1987) say, "It is apparently necessary that we have no knowledge of the processes by which our perceptual images are formed" (p. 88). When we understand that our minds construct these perceptions without conscious control, perhaps we will appreciate these processes and give up our belief that only consciously controlled, intentional processes are useful.

We see with the mind as well as the eye. What this means, among other things, is that when we look out of the same window, we do not necessarily see the same scene. We must examine these traditional ideas about the passive reception of information, because they have led us to teach as if we can *give* students an idea or concept.

Sensation, Perception, and the Brain

Current neuroscience has demonstrated that perception helps to shape the brain itself. Siegel (1999) says that "the human mind emerges from patterns in the flow of energy and information within the brain and between brains" (p. 2). We begin life with genetically "pre-programmed capacity for information processing." This capacity is in the form of modules specialized to handle certain kinds of information in very specific ways. Through experience, we build more and more complex modules capable of handling more complex information and ideas. We use the preprogrammed modules to build a brain.

The lowest level of experience, the level closest to the boundary between us and the external world, is sensation. Some neurons are specialized to construct representations of specific sensations, such as taste, touch, vision, and hearing. At this level, experience is far from thought. Categorization is minimal, and these experiences are difficult to describe in words. Layers of the sensory part of the brain serve as pattern-recognition modules. They fire when they detect a match. Repeated firing of sets of neurons creates an association between them, and they begin to act as a module. Even at this level, though, sensory representations are not just about the external world. They are constructed from information about the external world, the body, and the brain.

Perceptions are one level more complex than sensations. According to Siegel, perceptions are constructed from a synthesis of present sensations with past memory, generalizations, and emotion. Sensations and perceptions are the basis for more complex conceptual and categorical thought.

Over time, and with experience, children develop the ability to create ideas and to think about the mind itself. The ability to form these complex ideas allows children to begin to think about other people as separate from themselves. It allows them to form a concept of another person's mind, and to engage in social functions such as pretending. The mind operating at this level uses a categorical structure in which to classify and organize perceptual representations.

The development of language creates new capabilities, as we become able to share information about sensations, perceptions, and categories. This ability to share information is a great advance in our society and for each individual. Some theorists, according to Siegel, say that the development of language and the new form of consciousness that develops with it free us from the "remembered present" and allows us to think backward and forward in time. Vygotsky (1978) says that "the child begins to perceive the world not only through his eyes but also through his speech" (p. 32). Others say that this advanced form of consciousness comes from the development of the capacity to represent the self as experienced. In any case, this extremely advanced, higher form of consciousness allows us to understand minds in a complex way.

Learning Is an Action

Probably the most significant departure from passive notions of learning came about through the work of Jean Piaget and his colleagues. These researchers carefully observed and talked with children of various ages in a variety of settings related mostly to mathematical and scientific ideas. Piaget discovered, among other things, that children's thought is complex and quite different from adult thought. It is not different in the sense of being more primitive or simple. Rather, it is based on a different sort of logic, a different way of obtaining and dealing with information.

Even those who disagree with Piaget's theory or interpretations of his data have to admit that the children in his studies did not "see" things the way the adults did. One of his well-known studies, the conservation of liquid, shows young children pouring liquid from two identical containers into two dissimilar containers (one tall and narrow, the other short and wide). When the liquids are in the similar containers, the children report that the amount is the same in each. When the liquids are poured into the dissimilar containers, the children say that the amounts are different. This happens repeatedly even when the children pour the liquids themselves and no matter how many times they pour the liquids back and forth. Clearly, in this case, the children are not being "shown" that the liquids are the same. It appears so clear to adults and older children that it is hard to believe that the younger children are not seeing it.

We see with our mind, and, as Piaget established, part of what we see is determined by what we already think. Of course, we can, and do, change our mind, but our mind is not changed by someone showing us what we cannot see. That would be like trying to show a frog a fly at some angle that it cannot see, or trying to make a color-blind person see color.

What we can do, instead, is to provide conditions under which children can exercise their perceptual facilities. This is important in at least three ways:

1. Children need to learn what can be found out by direct contact between themselves and a phenomenon.
2. Children need sufficient experience in exploring various materials to form some intuitions about them.
3. Children need experience in discussing their perceptions with others and discovering the rich tapestry of experience that comes when people share genuine observations.

Experiment   *Experience*

Try this experiment yourself.* You will need two identical measuring cups, two identical containers of water, and two empty glasses. The glasses should be different shapes—one taller and thinner than the other. You will have to enlist some young children 3–5 years of age.

Seat each child, in turn, across from you at a table. While the child is watching, pour water into the two measuring cups to exactly the same level. When you have finished, ask the child whether the two cups have the same amount of water in them. Then pour the water from the measuring cup into one of the glasses. Pour from the other measuring cup into the other glass.

Ask the child, "If each of us is going to get one of the glasses to drink from, does it matter which one you get?" If the child says it does matter, ask why. If the child says that one has more, pour the contents of each glass back into its measuring cup and ask if one of them has more now.

Be sure to just ask, and then watch and listen carefully. Even though this might be difficult for you, please do not try to make the child see or convince him or her of the "right answer." Each of us eventually learns that a tall, thin glass does not hold more than a shorter, fatter one. For the child to hold a false belief for a while will not hurt.

*This experiment is fully described in Piaget's book *The Child's Conception of Number* (1965).

Learning from Direct Contact with the Phenomenon

A group of fourth graders were sitting in the sand preparing for a fossil dig. They had a grid to place on the sand and graph paper to chart the location of their finds. Some observers noticed that the children

did not seem to be paying attention to the instructions. They
appeared, in school vernacular, to
be "off-task." What was clear from
observing them was that they were
engaged in a different task: They
were investigating sand.

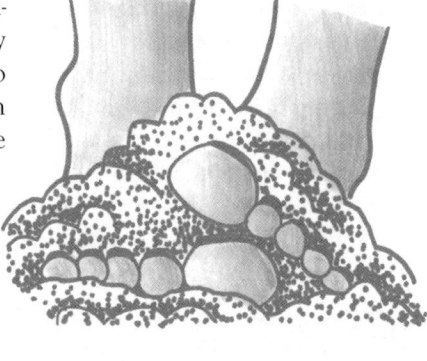

Some children had removed
their shoes and socks and were
burying their feet in the sand.
Some were sifting sand through
their fingers, and others were dripping sand from one hand to the
other. These children had to investigate sand before they could be
enticed into investigating the fossils. The same is true when children
and adults encounter materials that are new to them.

My colleague Kathleen Martin commented that children today seem
to have limited experiences with materials. We have had opportunities
to observe hundreds of children of all ages and backgrounds and found
that many children have not played with water and bubbles or played
in dirt, mud, or sand. Kathleen suggested that parents and teachers create containers of materials for children to investigate so they can develop perceptions of the materials in our world, which are essential foundational experiences for thought.

Some students at all ages, including high school and university,
have limited experiences with materials. In the past, most kids explored
the out-of-doors, played certain childhood games, took bubble baths,
and washed dishes. These common experiences created a uniformity of
background upon which teachers could build. These no longer are universal experiences. At all levels of education, we must be prepared to
provide experiences with objects, materials, and ideas for students who
have not had them.

Forming Bases for Intuitions

Perceiving provides a basis for further thought, giving us images with
which to think. Harvard psychologist Jerome Bruner (1956) writes about
the importance of thinking in images (which he calls "ikonic representation") as an essential phase of development. He believes, as does Piaget,
that a child first "thinks" in actions. Later the child learns to think in
images, which is part of development toward symbolic thought.

Dr. Ken Richardson, a mathematics professor at Texas Christian
University, says he often calls upon images of bubbles and other phenomena from his childhood when he tries to think about the mathe-

matical theories that are his research area. Richardson also says he cannot find a way to help students understand calculus if they do not have the experiences that allow them to *imagine* the calculus.

The experiences to which Richardson refers are not symbolic, mathematical experiences, but rather experiences with objects and materials. Thought begins in action and moves to intuition, imagination, and images. We then develop the ability to think in symbols, such as words. One important gift we can give children is to put them in the presence of rich perceptual experiences that will give them a foundation for the kind of images and intuitions they may develop.

Experiment *Experience*

Make some gloop.* Invite two to four children to investigate it with you. As you play with it, listen to the comments the children make to one another. Write a careful description of what you see and hear.

Gloop Recipe
1 1/2 cups room-temperature water
2 cups white school glue
Mix these two ingredients together until smooth. Add food coloring if you would like to color your gloop.

Mix:
1 tablespoon borax in 1 cup very warm water and pour into glue mixture, stirring constantly. The mixture will get gloopy. Grab a handful of the mixture and knead in your hands until the mixture is smooth and has lost its stickiness. Store in an airtight container. Continue to grab handfuls and knead until smooth.

It doesn't always work with the first batch. I've made It three times before it turns out just right.

Insiders tip: At times extra glue/water mixture will form at the bottom of the bowl. I take about a teaspoon of borax and add it to about 1/3 cup of warm water and mix it with the stuff in the bowl.

*This recipe is taken from Ross, M. E. (1995), *Sandbox Scientist* (Chicago: Chicago Review Press) as described by Anne Herndon, director of Hands On Science at the Fort Worth Museum of Science and History.

Discussing Perceptions

When I listen to parents, teachers, and students interacting with children and materials, these adults often focus on just naming things. They ask children to say the names of things, or the adults provide the children names of things.

Another kind of dialogue with children is often neglected: simply sharing what we see, hear, smell, taste, and feel, and listening carefully as they report what they see, hear, smell, taste, and feel. We need to be reminded of our sensory connection to the world. We tend to move so quickly to the conceptual that we at times forget to explore the materials first. As those fourth graders showed us, kids who are unfamiliar with sand need to wiggle their toes in it before they pick up pencil and paper to record their findings.

Discussing perceptions also creates a situation in which children have a way to figure out things for themselves. They do not have to remember a formula or a fact that someone else in this kind of setting has figured out. There are no wrong answers, and every now and then, as people share what they see, a picture emerges that is more than any one of us could have seen alone. When that happens, we collectively gain a sense of the power of shared vision that is a gift of being human.

Exploring New Environments

Neisser (1976) showed that we actively seek information from the environment; we hear a noise and turn our head. Babies engage in this active seeking of information. They seem to have an almost insatiable need to explore as soon as they are able to "get into things." As children grow older, adults frequently do not seem to recognize or encourage this need for children to explore. Actually, we tend to discourage it and act to constrain it.

As part of a class assignment, I asked my undergraduate college students to go to the local museum and write about their experience there. I then had them go back to the museum with a child on another day. The students were asked to simply follow the child and write down their observations. They were to answer any questions from the child but were not to direct the child in any way.

The undergraduates were amazed at the difference in the two experiences—their own and that of the child. Most of my students had not enjoyed the museum; they found it boring. Over the years that I have given this assignment, almost every one of them has said they "followed the path" and read the labels. Director of Interpretation for the museum, Charlie Walter, was present in class when we discussed the experience. I asked him if the museum had a "path," and he replied that it did not. He was surprised at the students' insistence of there being a path. The invisible path was a rigid boundary for my students, created by their experience of field trips to the museum, in which they had been asked to walk in a line in a defined way through the exhibits. Even the students who had not visited this museum previously believed it had a path because of their field trip experiences in other museums.

The children, in contrast, seemed to go to whatever captured them. To the undergraduates, they appeared to be "just running around." The undergraduates reported that the children were not "focused" and not "paying attention." The students were quite annoyed that I had asked them not to direct the children. The interesting and sad thing to me is that this belief persisted even when, from their own observations, the children clearly had enjoyed the visit immensely and had learned a great deal.

On another occasion, my class was observing children in a museum exhibit contained in one room. Again the children were free to go where they wished, and my undergraduates' assignment was to observe. This time I watched the movement of the children. I saw only one small group of girls who started at the beginning and looked at everything in order. These girls were the only ones who complained of being bored, finished early, and wished to leave. The others appeared to be randomly running here and there, like honeybees going from flower to flower. They looked briefly at everything, then went back and took the time to investigate more seriously certain things that interested them.

When one child found something interesting, he or she shouted or exclaimed, and other children usually came to see what was so interesting. This seemingly haphazard way of visiting the exhibit resulted in every child spending some time in every part of the exhibit, but not in any specific order. Colleen Blair, Director of School Services and Evaluation for the Fort Worth Museum of Science and History, said that this way of looking at everything and then going back to certain things is common in the museum world. She called it "shopping and browsing."

Exploring new environments in this way is a natural, adaptive, important part of being human. In any new place, the most sensible approach is to look it all over, then go to the things that interest us, saving the least interesting for last.

Learning to Trust Ourselves

We would do well to learn to trust ourselves again. We need to discover and follow our interests some of the time. Each of us is unique in background and experience. We have a contribution to make and a place to fill that is especially well suited to us.

I read about a tribe of people who celebrated when one of them became good at something. They followed what interested them. When one came forward to say that she had become good at weaving, for example, the tribe celebrated and changed the person's name to Mary Weaver.

As often as we can, I hope we will allow children to follow their interests and celebrate with them when they believe they have accomplished something. Like the students in the museum, too many of us are confined to an invisible path. Freeing ourselves and others to find our own way is worth the time and effort.

My friend Howard Polanz once said that the reason a circus elephant can be restrained by a rope around a leg is that it is first tied to a stake when it is very young and too weak to break the rope. By the time the elephant has grown strong enough to break the rope, it no longer tries.

We, too, are constrained by invisible bonds of assumptions about ourselves, about learning, and about knowledge. We don't have to stay on the path or read the labels. We don't have to continue reading a book just because we started it. We don't have to use up all of the shampoo we don't like before changing brands, or eat the banana that is overripe instead of one that is just right today.

Most young children have not yet lost touch with themselves. If we follow them, they show us a world we once knew and have forgotten. One of the joys of teaching is to be reminded of these things. I watched a group of young children exploring drops of water on waxed paper. They were fascinated with the way a water drop would merge into a neighboring drop if the two were close enough. Again and again they dropped a drop of water and then another at varying distances to see when they would merge. Until I watched them, I had forgotten how fascinating the experience of watching surface tension can be.

I hope we will begin to see the ways we create invisible paths that unnecessarily lead children away from themselves. Without intending to do so, we often impose order unnecessarily, without thinking about it, because it is the way we have always done it and we don't realize the harm it has caused. Perhaps we can trust the children and, in so doing, ourselves.

When my son was a sophomore in high school, his chemistry teacher commented that science is an objective way of investigating the world. My son asked, "What about the Heisenberg principle?" (This is the discovery by Heisenberg that the behavior of a photon is affected by the process of observing it.) The teacher dismissed his comment and went on with her lecture. If she had been willing to follow his thinking, class members might have engaged in a lively discussion that would have allowed them to see the complexity of an idea such as "objective." All the teacher needed to do was to ask him how he was thinking about that idea.

Exploration in Thought

O lder children and adults who have experience with objects and materials explore in a different way than those who do not have such experiences. As Piaget noted, the great advantage conferred by the development of cognition is that it frees us to think without having to actually *do* things. We can think about "what if"—and build mental models. We can imagine. We can even build new ideas in our mind that are not based on *direct* experience but instead are built from components of previous experiences. We can think about the past and the future. We can form hypotheses and mentally test them.

This ability is *potential* in the sense that it does not develop unless the person has had opportunities to engage in that kind of thought and to attempt to solve problems that *will* develop it. It is not just a matter of time. Time is involved to the extent that a person cannot rush the development of thought, but one can delay it.

I have done some of Piaget's experiments with people from wide age ranges, including adults. The older the people, the more variability the group has. The adult groups include some people who approach a problem in the same way as very young children, and others who approach a problem in sophisticated adult ways of thinking. Adults are capable of "what if" thought, but not in areas that are new to us.

I learned a variation of Piaget's experiment on volume, developed by Harvard Professor Eleanor Duckworth. A person is presented with a solid cube and a pile of small, square wooden blocks. He or she is told that a manufacturer of candy bars would like to make a bar with just as much candy as the cube but with a different shape. She then shows the person the new shape that the end of the candy bar will have to fit into, built using the small blocks. For example, if the original cube is 5″ × 5″ × 3″ and the end of it is 5″ × 5″, the new end might be 4″ × 4″ or 5″ × 3″ or some such configuration. The person is asked to build the new candy bar.

Most kindergartners who solve the problem build a cube that is the same height and length as the original cube, but with the new shape. Thus, their cube looks like the original but has fewer blocks. Older kids often do the same thing, but they know theirs is smaller and do not know what to do about it. Most third graders compensate for the smaller shape by adding more blocks to the length. Some adolescents and adults calculate precisely how much longer to make the bar so it has *exactly* as much chocolate as the original.

What is interesting is that, though no kindergartner acts like an adult, some adults solve the problem in the same way as kids of each age. Thus, development seems to put a kind of constraint on what we are able to think, but it does not guarantee that we will think a certain way just because of our age.

Exploration in Conversation

nother form of exploration is *conversation*. Conversation is not the same as talking. It offers the opportunity to truly listen to another and respond. The ability to explore by sharing and hearing *thoughts* is an extension of exploration by examining things.

In very young children, of course, the ability to converse is absent. Teachers have reported to me that in first grade, if the entire class is working on a problem—such as finding patterns in a number chart—each child has to see and say it for himself or herself. If Mary says, "The numbers in the second row all start with one," each child will repeat his or her observation of that pattern when he or she sees it. In third grade, if a second child repeats what someone said already, many of the children will respond, "We already said that." They have learned to share thoughts and work as a unit so what is shared belongs to the group. In a sense, they have built a mind that is made up of all the other minds.

Attending

We all know what it means to be asked to "pay attention." When I was in college, I had a habit of thinking about other things while I walked to class. One day I walked right into the side of a parked car. I was late to class and later discovered, to my embarrassment, that the whole class had been watching me out the window. My professor told me to pay attention. When I was reprimanded to pay attention, I knew that she meant that I should quit paying attention to what I was attending to and attend to something else instead. I did not walk into the parked car because I was incapable of attending, or even because I wasn't attending, but, rather, because I was attending to something else.

What we call *attention* is a process or a habit of focusing. At any moment in time, a number of things are happening in and around me. Of all these, I am aware of only a few. The rest, including some complex thought processes, are occurring without my conscious awareness.

Most of us turn our head in response to a loud noise. That is not an indication of interest; it is the kind of environmental condition that commands our attention. We use expressions such as "it caught my eye" to indicate that other, less startling environmental conditions also demand our attention. What tends to catch our attention is something new or unexpected, a change of some sort. Because we all have different experiences and different knowledge, we also have different expectations. What is novel to you might not be novel to me.

One phenomenon in psychology is called the *novelty effect*. It refers to our attending to new things and then, when we become accustomed to them, not attending any more. I drive from my house to the university on automatic pilot. If I'm going somewhere else in that general direction, I sometimes end up at the university without meaning to. What amazes me is that I can drive unconsciously, and apparently do so safely. I go into my mind, and if something unexpected happens, I come back.

Jokes make use of this novelty effect. They violate our expectations, and if we are too inexperienced to have expectations, a joke isn't funny. Mary Ann, a teacher, told me that kindergartners are not interested in books such as the Amelia Bedelia books, in which the humor is about inconsistencies. Children don't see the discontinuities; the novelty isn't funny. Veteran teachers know when to introduce these books. Their experience has taught them that children are not able to respond to these books earlier.

The psychologist E. C. Cherry (1953) conducted an interesting study on attention. In this formal experiment, participants were asked to pay attention to a sound broadcast to one ear, while unrelated sounds were broadcast to the other ear. Even when the unrelated sound was a single word repeated 35 times, the participants had no memory of it. When a participant's name was mentioned once, he or she shifted attention immediately.

What we call attention is actually a complex relationship of conscious and unconscious divisions of duties. Having opportunities to learn to attend is just as important as having opportunities to learn to explore.

In one of our studies with teachers, we investigated how teachers of young children (kindergarten through third grade) make judgments about children's mathematical knowledge. We found that one of the ways they decide that a child knows something is that they see the child do it or comment about it repeatedly. For example, one teacher described teaching an A-B pattern in mathematics. The child saw the pattern in a spelling word later in the day, and in a piece of clothing.

The teachers in the study said they had thought that children who were learning about patterns needed to practice until they learned them. Now they understood that teachers can watch to see whether the patterns spring up spontaneously, which indicates that the children understand. Similarly, teachers have a tendency to think that we must force children to pay attention so they will become engaged with a phenomenon or an idea, when what really happens is that when children find something engaging, they tend to become focused. We don't have to force them to pay attention; attention is a natural consequence of our interest.

Trying to force ourselves to "pay attention" doesn't seem to work. Even when we are listening to an interesting story, we often go off on tangents, taking little excursions in our mind. As a result of thinking about the mind as if it were a machine, we have developed the notion that commanding attention is a good thing, that the ability to focus is important in and of itself. Attending is important in the context of what we attend to and what we do with what we learn. If, when we really want to, we can't seem to quiet our mind long enough to focus on something of interest to us, and if that happens often enough to interfere with our life and enjoyment, we might want to seek help. Most of us do not have that trouble daily.

In the United States today, much concern has been generated about children who seem to have difficulty attending. The number of children assumed to have deficiencies in the ability to attend is large enough to be of grave concern. The number of children diagnosed with attention deficit hyperactivity disorder (ADHD) in the past decade has increased dramatically. Part of the reason for this could be that we do not create conditions that promote habits of attending.

Focal attention, the ability to bring an idea or experience into working memory, is important. Initially, Siegel (1999) says, an event has meaning for an individual because "it is discrepant from prior experiences or because other evaluative processes label it with significance" (p. 126). The first case, in which an event is meaningful because it is discrepant from prior experience, is one that Piaget discussed at some length. Siegel says that the brain is an anticipation machine. Piaget described the importance of surprise in the development of children's thought. When we form an idea about how a sequence of events will occur and they do not occur that way, we are surprised and we focus on that sequence and try to figure out what is wrong with our idea or what went wrong in the sequence of events. This is one of the occasions in which, Siegel says, our emotions alert the brain to focus attention. He says that this leads to increased alertness and energy. But it is not the end of the story. If we hear a sudden loud noise, orient to it, and discover it was a car backfiring, we return to our previous state and activities. We have experienced Siegel's second element in focusing attention, which is that there is further appraisal of "the meaning of the stimulus and of the aroused state itself" (p. 126). These emotional appraisal and arousal processes prepare us to act in a certain fashion. They can not be simulated by the command "pay attention" coming from outside ourselves.

Interest Versus Effort

In his essay "Interest and Effort in Education" (Boydston, 1980), John Dewey discusses the debate that arose about the value of interest in education. He says that one side of the debate holds that life is full of things that are not interesting and children need to learn to expend effort in dealing with these things anyway. On the other hand:

> It is absurd to suppose that a child gets more intellectual or mental discipline when he goes at a matter unwillingly than when he goes at it out of the fullness of his heart. The theory of effort simply says that unwilling attention (doing something disagreeable because it is disagreeable) should take precedence over spontaneous attention. (Boydston, 1980, p. 153)

Dewey points out that education has taken up both positions in ways that place "the object, idea or end to be mastered" outside the self. It is assumed that, *after* subject matter is selected, it has to be *made* interesting or that an act of will is required to engage it. Dewey suggests something more in line with my observations of children. He says that a student becomes genuinely interested when, in the course of taking some action, an object or idea becomes necessary to continue the action.

Creating Situations That Engage Children

We do not create enough situations in which children are caught up in something that engages them. We interrupt children regularly and ask them to make sudden and intrusive shifts. This is particularly true of schools, where learning is governed by clock time and children are interrupted many times throughout the day to move—and attend—to some other subject.

Attending takes time. One of the things we have been able to do in our space in the museum is simple, yet powerful: We allow children to finish. Children become interested to different degrees and in different things. One day a group of third-grade pupils were building with flat, rectangular, wooden blocks. One boy named Raul obviously was more engaged than the others. He was building a complex structure and was concentrating so hard that even his classmates' comments went unanswered. The only thing that seemed to distract him was when someone came close enough to threaten his structure. On that day, none of the others was that engaged by building, and they all finished within the time we had allotted. We gave this boy a large supply of blocks and let him continue while the others went on to something else. After a time, Raul said, "There!" and walked away. The satisfied look on his face was delightful.

In a usual school situation, the boy would have had to put away the blocks when the allotted time was up. Without intending to, we would have interrupted his con-centration and his habit of attending. Many teachers believe that they must "cover" the curriculum and that they do not have time to allow children to finish. They insist that children stop what they are doing before they are finished so they can move on to the next thing and stay on schedule. Sometimes the children pretend to stop and then go back to the activity as soon as the teacher moves on, but more often they put it away.

When teachers think about what this does to children, some teachers rethink the structure of their classrooms and make different choices. Teachers sometimes allow a child to continue working while the rest of the class moves on to something else. Some let a particularly engaged child finish his or her immediate task and then go back later to work on the project. Others allow a child to take the materials home and continue working on them there. Often, allowing an engaged child to finish involves only a relatively short time. Yet, this is helpful to the child and frees him or her to be fully present for the next task.

We need to create conditions for children to develop habits of attending that will serve them well as thinkers and learners. These conditions include interesting, engaging, enticing environments, as well as freedom from interference and protection from interruption. I am not arguing that people always should be able to do what is interesting to them. At times we need to do things for other reasons. Sometimes we have to interrupt children and ask them to do things because they are part of a group and their own interest must be set aside. What I am asking is that we understand the impact of those interruptions and be more thoughtful about when and how we interrupt.

Children's exploration has to be followed at some point by attending. We can create interesting settings, allow children to explore, and expect that something will engage them. If this does not happen, we can assume that the environment we have created, though it might be rich enough for the students who are attending, might not be rich enough for those who are not.

Sometimes the problem is not in the conditions. A child might come to us with a history of "glancing instead of looking," as Kathleen Martin says. Mary, a middle school girl, spent about 10 minutes glancing through an environment. She went over to a staff member, Lisa, and said she was "finished" and "bored" and wanted something else to do. Lisa told her that they were going to be there for 2 hours and that it was up to Mary to decide how she would spend that time, but there would be no other things to do and Mary could not leave or disrupt the other students. Mary went back and looked at some things again. Something caught her attention, and she became engaged by it.

No one proper response or diagnosis is to be had. A teacher who knows the children well will be able to determine how to respond. Sometimes, though, we are too quick to assume that the problem is *in* the child, without assuming that we can help the child to overcome that problem. As Jerome Bruner (1990) says, our biology does not determine our behavior. It constrains it. Culture is, and always has been, about overcoming these constraints. Some children have more difficulty focusing or attending than others do. The former are the children who most need help in learning to overcome these constraints.

When I see a child who is thoroughly engaged with some phenomenon—such as Raul, the child building with the blocks—it tells me something important about the child. It helps me to see an inclination that can be encouraged, nurtured, and fed. What often happens instead is that the child is encouraged to do something else in a well-meaning, but unfortunate, attempt to help him or her to become more "well rounded."

Patrick was a third grader who was earning B's in all of his classes. His teacher was concerned because, although Patrick was an exceptional artist, she believed he was interested only in art. The referring teacher wanted Patrick evaluated for ADHD. I submit that most of us would be happy if we could find one thing that we love and do well and could be above average the rest of the time. We would not consider ourselves to have a disorder. It is also true that children vary in their ability to focus attention. Those in whom this ability is so limited that it disrupts their lives require, and should be given, special assistance. But these children are relatively rare.

We have different expectations of children than we do of adults. We want children to be interested in what we provide for them. What we often get in return are children who learn to *look* interested. University students in general are people who have done well in school. Look through the windows into some lecture classes at a university, and you will see large numbers of students *looking* interested. If you interview them as they walk out, though, you will often find that some of them are no more in the room than I am in the car when I drive to work. We can't *make* people attend. We can *create conditions* wherein they probably will attend to something. We can assume that, like most people, children have differing interests. Sometimes those different interests can be accommodated, and sometimes they can't. Although children need to do some things that do not interest them, they probably will not do them as well—just like adults do.

Brenda, a kindergarten teacher, liked to read to the children. She had them sit on the floor in front of her quietly as she read. She told me that they could not pay attention to the story unless they sat quietly like that. I asked her to find out if that was true. She read a story the next day and allowed the children to move around as much as they wished. Then she asked them questions about the story. She was astonished to find that the children had heard the story even though they appeared not to be paying attention. She also learned that the reason she liked them to sit in front of her was that *she* was distracted by their moving around.

That was a good enough reason to ask them to sit. Classrooms, after all, must be comfortable for teachers as well as students, and teachers who understand their own needs may be better able to accommodate the needs of their students. Once she understood the real reason for her request, Brenda was able to ask the children to sit still enough for her comfort level without having to insist on their being absolutely still.

People are natural learners. Learning is a part of our deep connection to and resonance with nature. Deep within us is a need to explore, attend, investigate, understand, and know. We are sense makers. Learning is gratifying. Figuring things out, solving problems, and making things is as much a part of who we are as blood and bone. If children lose touch with their need to make sense of things, they will have lost touch with an important part of what it means to be human.

Summary

Without our awareness or control, we create the sensations that make up our world. Our senses connect us to the world and provide the raw data that we use to construct the immediate experiences that we use to think with. Therefore, exploration of places, objects, and materials is an important part of growing up. Exploration also involves engagement, in which we attend to and focus on certain aspects of an environment. Though we cannot command or force children to "pay attention," we can create conditions that help children to develop habits of attending.

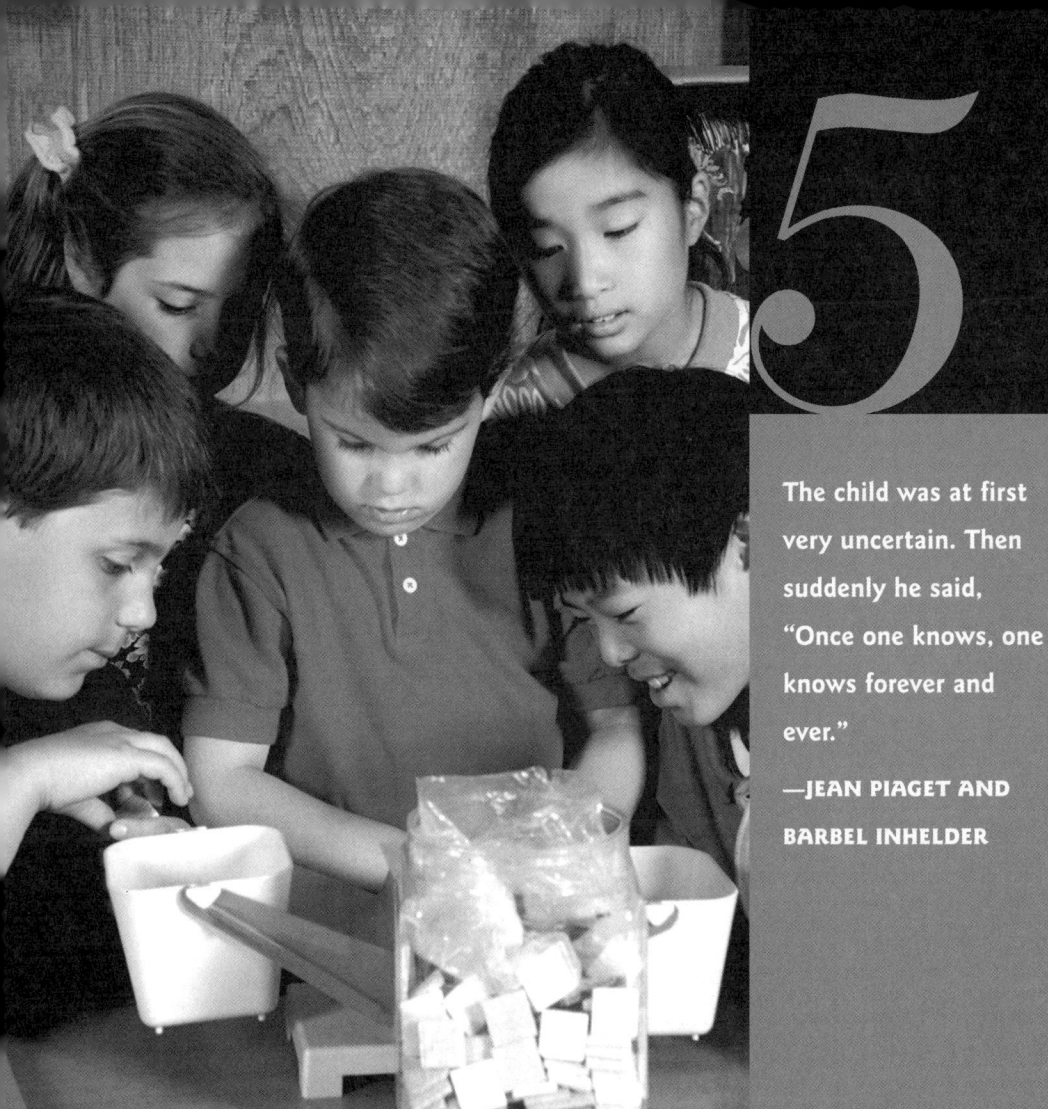

The child was at first very uncertain. Then suddenly he said, "Once one knows, one knows forever and ever."

—JEAN PIAGET AND BARBEL INHELDER

Learning, Remembering, and Understanding

I n the brief historical review in Chapters 1 and 2, we explored the dramatic shift in thought as we began to move into the Post-Modern era. One of the most important turning points in that shift for teachers and parents was the work led by Jean Piaget. He was a Swiss scholar who began his professional life as a zoologist, publishing his first paper in that field as a young adolescent. He studied clinical psychology for a time and worked with Binet, who was developing the new intelligence test (which eventually became the Stanford-Binet test, still in use today).

As he was testing children, Piaget noticed that often children got the wrong answer for the right reason or the right answer for the wrong reason. He became interested in the ways that children reason and ultimately developed a theory of knowledge that he called a "genetic epistemology." Jerome Bruner says of Piaget: "His passions were epistemology and logic and how they grew by the actions of the growing child on the world" (1983, p. 137). Although he was not trying to write a new view of development, Piaget's pursuit of genetic epistemology unearthed some patterns in children's thought that challenged some deep fundamental ideas about children, learning, and teaching.

A problem for Piaget, and for us, is to figure out how people and animals develop, how we change over time. Babies learn to do things that are appropriate for their species. Not only do the young learn from the previous generations, but they also extend that knowledge and add to it, so that species, and the individuals within it, grow and change. We could almost say that we are made for learning.

As discussed in Chapter 3, recent studies in the development of the human brain appear to indicate that the brain develops throughout life and that this development is inextricably tied to experience (Greenough, Black, & Wallace, 1987; Nowakowski, 1987). According to Greenough and colleagues (1987, p. 543), humans, and many other species, "seem to have evolved such that the genes need only roughly outline the pattern of neural connectivity in a sensory system, leaving the more specific details to be determined through the organism's interaction with its environment."

Processes like learning, remembering, and understanding are called "cognition." Studies of cognition have focused on the *acquisition* of information, knowledge and skills, and *retention* (memory and the development of habits). Although these have been treated as separate research topics, from a teacher's perspective they are inseparable. Perhaps even more important for teachers and parents is to know how understanding develops, how we might aid in the growth of understanding, and how the experiences of students help to build a brain.

Modernist Ideas About Learning

The study of learning has occupied psychologists for many years. The earliest form of learning identified by researchers, as pointed out in Chapter 1, was a primitive phenomenon called conditioning. You will recall that "classical conditioning" is the name given to a form of conditioning demonstrated by the Russian researcher Pavlov. He used an already existing association between a stimulus and a response. He knew that hungry dogs salivate in the presence of food and do not salivate when they hear a bell. Pavlov demonstrated that dogs could learn, or be conditioned, to salivate when a bell is rung. He did this by repeatedly pairing the ringing of the bell with the presentation of food. At some point the dogs began to salivate at the sound of the bell even when no food was present.

Other pioneers of learning theory explored similar ideas about learning. Most of the work during the Modern period was done with animals, usually mice or rats, and involved learning to negotiate a maze of some kind. Research focused on how learning develops by looking for the mechanisms present at birth and attempting to account for the ways in which people use these mechanisms to develop into adults. Researchers justified making inferences from animals to people on the basis of the similarity between their nervous systems.

The most enduring learning theories from this period were those associated with behaviorism in one of its various forms. Even though behaviorism is not the dominant theory any more, it retains a strong foothold in schools and in our culture.

The root of the behaviorist learning theory is the idea of instrumental conditioning. As discussed in Chapter 1, this form of conditioning, unlike Pavlov's classical conditioning, does not begin with a physiologically established stimulus-response pair such as salivating in the presence of food. Instrumental conditioning focuses on reinforcement.

If a response to a stimulus leads to a positive reinforcement reward, the bond between the two is strengthened and the probability of that response being emitted in the presence of that stimulus increases. A reward is an individual thing. It must be something rewarding to the individual. To a hungry mouse, for example, food is rewarding. To a mouse that is not hungry, food is not rewarding.

One of the ways that the pioneers of learning theory were able to ensure that the mouse would respond to the reward was to deprive it of food for a certain time prior to the experiment and then offer the food as a reward. The food-deprived mouse is considered to be motivated to seek food when it follows a maze to try to reach the food.

The notion of motivation has some appeal because earlier ways of speaking about goal seeking used concepts such as "will" and "intention." These ideas were too "mentalistic" for behaviorists, whereas motivation could be defined operationally as the number of days of food deprivation; it could be controlled by the experimenter; and it could be studied by observation alone (watching a rat seek food). Therefore, it was more acceptable than an internal experience such as will or intent.

As a result of this way of thinking about motivation, the word "motivation," which originally referred to an internal state, was changed to refer to something that occurred from outside.

Many behaviorists assumed that, beyond some primitive reflexes present at birth, all that becomes known in a lifetime is built up through these reinforced stimulus-response pairings. The behaviorists abandoned this idea fairly early, because even on the face of it, they ascertained that this one idea cannot account for the vast, complex array of knowledge. Mainstream psychology has heavily criticized and largely abandoned behaviorism as a viable learning theory.

On the other hand, behaviorism has been, and is, useful in animal training and still is commonly used in schools under the aegis of "classroom management." Various ways of maintaining discipline and order have evolved from ideas about rewarding desired behavior and withholding rewards from behaviors that teachers wish to change. The persistence of this theory and its application stems not from a belief in behaviorism as a learning theory but, rather, from its utility as a short-term control of undesirable behavior.

Remembering

Remembering is an important facet of knowing. Obviously, knowing something is useful only if we can remember it. Memory is not simply a matter of retrieving information previously stored, however. For many years we treated memory and learning as if the brain were a large filing cabinet into which information could be placed for later retrieval. Siegel (1999), summarizing current literature on memory and brain development, says that memory is better thought of as reconstructed rather than retrieved. Gruber and Vonèche (1995) report on one of Piaget's experiments with a group of children who were at one level of development. Then he went back later, when the children had moved to the next level of development, and asked them to describe the experiment. They described it as if they had participated in it at their current level of functioning, even though they had not seen the experiment since the previous experience. In this sense, all memory is revisionist. Memories are constructed from subsequent as well as prior events.

A good deal of research has been done on memory, trying to account for why we remember some things and not others and why we remember something for a while and then forget it. Information-processing theories use computers as a metaphor for thinking about how the mind works. Atkinson and Shiffren (1968) developed one of the best known information-processing "storage" theories. They propose three different kinds of memory stores: sensory register, short-term memory, and long-term memory.

1. *Sensory register* is the initial intake of data through the senses. It is considered to be transient and easily disrupted. Sensory data that are not attended to or moved to short-term storage are assumed to dissipate.
2. *Short-term memory (STM)* is considered to be a way of remembering for a longer time, but not permanently. It has a limited capacity, both in terms of the amount of storage available and the duration of the storage. Memories in STM dissipate in time.
3. *Long-term memory (LTM)* is considered to be relatively limitless. Information stored in LTM is assumed to be stored permanently.

Control processes are strategies and habits that allow us to overcome the limitations of STM or to enhance the probability of transfer to LTM. One strategy is *rehearsal*, in which a person repeats information again and again. Rehearsal is considered to keep the memory refreshed and prevent dissipation. This is what we do, for example, in order to remember a phone number if we have to look it up in one location and walk to a phone in another location. The fragility of this form of memory can be seen by the way we forget the number if someone or something interrupts us on the way.

We use another kind of brief remembering frequently in school and school-like settings. Just before a test over chapters in a textbook, students often read a few note cards or papers before going into the classroom and try to hold on to the facts long enough to write them on the test. If someone speaks to them in the interim, they might lose the knowledge they were trying to remember. A week later they usually remember very little of that information. If they are tested again over the same material a month later, without reviewing it, they very well could fail the test. The motto has been said to be "cram and release."

Yet another strategy for brief remembering is to read over the chapters in the text several times the night before the exam. Many students say they perform best on multiple-choice exams by learning the material in only a superficial way. One of my students, Jennifer, said:

I crammed so much information in my head before those tests that when I left the lab, it was like letting the air out of a balloon. . . . After that test, a great pressure was lifted from me. I know now that the material I had memorized left me too.

Many of us use aids in reconstructing memories to get through exams. When I studied neurology, I had to memorize the names of all the facial nerves. An older student taught me a memory device that had been passed down from student to student through the years: On Old Olympus Towering Top A Finn And German Viewed Some Hops. I still remember the aid, but I do not remember the names of the nerves! I probably can reconstruct most of them, however, by thinking about the letters in the memory aid. It would take time, but it isn't completely lost.

Beyond Brief Memory

Forgetting is as important in life as remembering. Clearly, we do not want to remember everything we've experienced. But, for the most part, teachers want students to remember and understand some things rather than remember for just a short time or have a vague sense of having been exposed to something, or even be able to reconstruct it from some sort of memory device. This requires a different approach.

One way to overcome memory limitations was discovered by George Miller (1956), who found that memory is limited to 5 ± 2 chunks of information. If we try to remember five unrelated things, these will be limited to short-term memory. But if we combine information into meaningful packets, each packet counts as one "chunk." This is related to the idea of the information-processing theorists: Memory is enhanced by meaningful processing.

We use this idea, perhaps without thinking about how or why it works, in our daily life. We teach children the letters of the alphabet by making a song out of them. We tell children stories as a way of helping them to understand or convey information. In fact, according to Jerome Bruner (1956, 1973, 1983, 1990), narrative is the most fundamental form of human understanding, so it makes sense that we remember stories.

When I want students to remember and, later, be able to use what they know, I ask them to talk or write about the ideas as they relate to their experience. Sometimes I have them make observations and bring in what they saw. Then we work together to find the patterns in their data. I follow this by telling them about the relevant findings of researchers. I find that students are better able to remember this way. The information-processing theorists would attribute this to the way the information is processed. Bruner would say that it makes the information more meaningful.

The bulk of current evidence suggests that there is more than one kind of memory. Typically, memory is divided at least into semantic and episodic memory. According to Siegel (1999), "semantic memory is a type in which we can recall factual information, such as the capitals of the major countries of Europe" (p. 39). Episodic recall is more autobiographical and "evokes a process of mental time travel—the sense of the self in time—which differentiates it from semantic recollections" (p. 39).

Episodic memory, Siegel says, is developed in early family relationships. He suggests that children who have "elaborative relationships" with their parents and who talk about their experiences with their parents recall more details about their lives later on. "Elaborative parents talk with their children about what they, the children, think about the stories they read together. In contrast, 'factual' parents—the classification designating parents who are found to talk only about the facts of stories, not a child's imagination or response—have children with a less developed ability for recall" (1999, p. 45).

The implications of this for parents and teachers are clear. If we are trying to help children build a brain, we will engage children in conversation about their experiences before, during, and after an event or experience. When we read or engage in an experiment, or walk outside to observe the weather, we will encourage children to elaborate on their comments and converse with us and each other about what they see and understand and how that relates to prior experiences.

Current literature on the effects of emotion on memory (Damasio, 1994; Siegel, 1999) suggest that emotion directs memory in the sense that experiences with little emotional intensity are less likely to be considered important and less likely to be remembered. Siegel (1999) cites studies that have demonstrated that "if the brain appraises an event as 'meaningful', it will be more likely to be recalled in the future" (p. 48).

If you've ever watched children playing video games, you have seen an example of the way memory is shared among friends. A group that plays together often has a self-organizing shared memory and skills. When children get to a certain point in a game, they hand the controller to the child who has the most knowledge or skill for that point in the game.

Malcolm Gladwell (2002) described an experiment on shared memory by Wegner. Fifty-nine couples who had been dating for at least 3 months participated. Half of the couples stayed with their partners and the other half were paired with someone they didn't know. All of the pairs then read 64 statements, "each with an underlined word, like 'midori is a Japanese melon liqueur.'" The pairs were allowed to read the statements for 5 minutes and were then asked to write down as many of the statements as they could remember. The pairs who knew each other remembered substantially more items than the pairs who didn't know each other. Gladwell reports that "when people know each other well, they create an implicit joint memory system . . . which is based on an understanding about who is best suited to remember what kinds of things" (2002, p. 188).

The more recent information-processing theories emphasize *levels* of processing as the key to memory. Information that is processed superficially decays and is forgotten quickly. Information that is processed meaningfully and is linked with knowledge currently in the system is retained for a longer time.

Extended Memory

Ever since the invention of writing, people have been able, in a sense, to extend memory by recording thoughts and consulting the notes later. This extends storage capability both individually and culturally. I extend my own storage by recording and later referring to my notes. I also gain the ability, to some extent, to share in others' memories when I read what they have written. Bruner (1990) says:

> As Roy Pea, David Perkins, and others now put it, a "person's" knowledge is not *just* in one's own head, in "person solo," but in the notes that one has put into accessible notebooks, in the books with underlined passages on one's shelves, in the handbooks one has learned how to consult, in the information sources one has hitched up to the computer, in the friends one can call up to get a reference or a "steer," and so on almost endlessly. All of these, as Perkins points out, are parts of the knowledge flow of which one has become a part. (p. 106)

Understanding

According to the *Oxford English Dictionary*, one form of the word "understand" means "to step under." Stepping under an idea is not the same thing as acquiring, retaining, and using information. Understanding means knowing how things work, how they go together. Through understanding, we build intellectual tools that we can use with many different kinds of content.

The history of science shows us the kind of progress that can be made as a result of inventing new tools. The telescope and the microscope literally opened up new worlds that had not been seen previously. The history of science also shows us that ideas have opened up new worlds that we could not see until those ideas came along. Piaget and Garcia (1991) wrote about this interesting parallel between the development of ideas in science and the development of ideas in an individual.

Development of the intellect enables people to move from manipulating objects in the external world to representing the external world in symbols and signs that can be manipulated in thought. This is faster and easier. It is what makes true invention possible. If we believe that the goal of teaching is for children to develop the ability to think, create, invent, and generally to go beyond what is currently known, we must understand how true understanding occurs and how the mind can be developed to its full potential.

One of the obstacles to understanding is rooted in the empiricist view of the relationship between our thought and the world outside of us. This view—which was held for many years and is still fairly common today—is that a "real" world exists outside of us and we copy it in our mind as closely as possible, reproducing it in the form of an idea that is as much like the original as possible. To an empiricist, knowledge is the reproduction of the observable.

Piaget says that this view is untenable, that knowledge is not impressed upon a child like an image on a photographic plate. Knowledge comes from the interactions between us and the world. We do not receive or acquire knowledge, Piaget maintains. Instead, we act on the world around us, based on our current ideas and ability to think, and the world acts on us and our ideas and ability to think. This interaction between us and the external environment is what creates and refines ideas and develops our ability to reason and think. Support for this idea has come from neurological studies demonstrating the role of experience in brain development (Greenough, Black, & Wallace, 1987; Nowakowski, 1987).

Appearance and Reality

Thinking about how we construct ideas about the external world leads us to wonder whether babies see the world as we do. Piaget became interested in that question. "He asked whether the child, in its first months of life, conceives and perceives things as we do, as objects that have substance, that are permanent and of constant dimensions" (Gruber & Vonèche, 1995, p. 250). Piaget wondered whether babies know that a thing exists even when they cannot see it. His studies led him to believe that this notion is constructed early in life and is not inborn. In Piaget's view, we are not restricted to our biological, inborn nature; we elaborate and build upon that nature, constructing new intellectual tools.

In studies with young babies, Piaget hid an object behind a screen while the baby was watching. He observed that very young infants act as if the object has disappeared and do not look for it. Piaget suggested that this is because babies have not yet developed *object permanence*; they do not yet know that objects exist even when they cannot see them. The idea of object permanence is one of the "mental operations" that Piaget believed we must construct. Mental operations are a set of tools that we can use in subsequent thought.

Piaget and his collaborators studied children of all ages in many countries, presenting them with new problems that they had not seen before. The researchers observed how children solved problems and how they explained the solutions. In more than 50 years of research, Piaget said he was astonished that children from the same environment and age gave more or less the same answers, even though they were asked questions they had not thought about before. This remarkable similarity among children in the way they think in a novel situation led Piaget to believe that children's thought has a structure to it (Piaget, 1977).

In his famous conservation experiment, which was discussed in Chapter 4, Piaget poured liquid from a beaker into two identical measuring cups, filling each to exactly the same point. You will recall that he asked the child to verify that the two cups each had the same amount. Then he poured from each measuring cup into a dish while the child watched. One dish was short and wide and the other was tall and thin. Young children said that one dish (usually the taller one) had more. Then, with the child watching, Piaget poured the water from both dishes back into the measuring cups. The child then thought both containers had the same amount of water. No matter how many times the liquid was poured back and forth, the child responded the same. This response was consistent in children of the same age.

We have a hard time believing that a child who sees the equal amounts of liquid being poured into the dishes cannot "see" that they hold the same amount. The child can "see" that no liquid was added or taken away, but he or she can't "see" it in a way that leads to the conclusion that the amount of liquid is the same when it doesn't look the same. What appears to us to be a simple fact actually requires some rather sophisticated mental operations that must be developed.

Piaget showed us that the *ability* to override perception with logic develops over time, but it does not mean that the *action* of overriding perception with logic necessarily develops. What allows us to know the world is not our direct perception, but the mental operations we are able to perform. Most of these mental operations must be constructed in the course of cognitive growth.

Assimilation

When we eat something, say an apple, the apple becomes part of us. We take in the apple, digest it, transform it. Part of the apple stays with us, and the parts we cannot currently use are discarded. Once we have eaten the apple, it is so transformed that we cannot find its unique contribution separate from the rest of us.

Piaget believes that this biological process, called *assimilation,* is a good metaphor for the relationship between us and the knowledge that we construct. New ideas do not come to us from the outside unchanged. We assimilate and deform the external information and incorporate it into ourselves according to the way we are able to use it and organize it. What we cannot currently use, we discard. Like the apple, the new ideas and information become so much a part of what was there before that they are not identifiable in their original form. The more we think about and use ideas, the more we incorporate them into the way we see things, which always changes them in some way.

Assimilation is a conservation process in the sense that it preserves, to a certain extent, what is there already. It is a way of trying to fit the new idea into old ideas without changing the old very much, if at all. In spite of this tendency to conserve, the process of assimilating the new idea also opens up new possibilities.

In teaching, we have to learn to follow children. "Following children" means that we observe carefully and intervene in what a child is doing only when we have a clear sense of how the child is currently thinking and what might help him or her to think or act differently. This is a different way of being with children for most people, and it is not what my students think they should be doing as teachers. Many of them think that teaching is about giving information and correcting errors. Most believe that teaching is a bag of tricks wherein we learn methods that work and then do these with our students.

To illustrate, here is an excerpt from a paper that Mark Grossman wrote about his first experience with learning to follow, by doing a conservation experiment with a kindergartner:

> My heart was pounding as I walked into the cafeteria; I did not exactly know what to do or how I should act. I have had absolutely no experience with children. . . .

Grossman then explained the problem to the child and wrote about what the child did next:

> At first D took some cubes and built up a bar that was the equal size to the original bar. He asked if that was equal size, and I told him that they looked equal. . . . D finished his next piece and showed it to me. It was a bar of four squares as I had asked, but it was only as long as the original bar.
>
> This was the first snag that I encountered, but I had thought a great deal about the problem, so I was prepared for something like this. I wanted D to see what was wrong without telling him, so I asked him if

he thought they, the original and the bar he had just made, had the same amount of chocolate. D shook his head and said, "No, this one [the original] has more chocolate." I asked him if there was any way to keep the end of four and have the same amount of chocolate. D said yes and went back to working to show me how. (personal communication)

In the beginning, many teacher education students try to assimilate the idea of following a child to their already established and deeply ingrained ideas about teaching. This is evidenced in statements that reflect their belief that following a child is a method or a procedure to be followed. Some even ask for a set of steps to follow. Even with these erroneous ideas, as they attempt to follow what seems to them to be a method, they begin to notice things about what the child is doing, which opens the possibility of their actually understanding what it means to follow a child's thought. In this way, without their awareness, they are living Piaget's ideas about assimilation.

Accommodation

Even as we try to assimilate something new, the external world resists assimilation; it doesn't support just any idea. If I sit in a chair and act as if it is a car, it still won't take me any place because the chair resists the idea that it is a car. This resistance by the external world leaves me with two choices: to reject the environmental event, or to modify my way of thinking. This modification of thought is what Piaget called accommodation.

In the conservation-of-liquid experiment, I have seen children who are convinced that the amount of liquid in the measuring cups is the same and that the containers into which it is poured contain different amounts. These children are certain of what they think. They do not deal with the contradiction; they reject the external event. When my students questioned the children about where the "extra" water came from, many of them said, "It's magic." One child decided that one of the measuring cups must have more liquid, even though they looked the same, because he was certain that the container had more liquid.

Other children are certain that the liquid is the same in both containers and say things like, "All you did was pour it, so if it was the same in the measuring cups, it is the same now." If pressed to explain, they reason that, although one container is taller, and thus seems to hold more, it also is thinner, so the liquid just "pushed up more."

The children who accommodate do some fascinating things. One child, Bobby, filled both containers to the same height, then poured the water back into the measuring cups. When he saw that one of the measuring cups now held more than the other, he reasoned that the containers were just shaped differently.

To have all of the children repeat Bobby's experiment so they would all "see" would be tempting but it would not work. This experiment helped Bobby because he was testing an idea. When the external environment did not support his idea, he was able to give it up. He then was open to another idea.

Creating Conditions to Support Assimilation and Accommodation

Assimilation and accommodation are facets of a single intellectual process that is supported by different conditions. We can create environments in which these conditions are present. For example, we have given schoolchildren sets of materials such as various kinds of paper plates, cups, bowls, flat-bottomed screws, and pointed dowels. The children were asked to construct a top that would spin a long time. Most of the children selected a plate of some kind and put a dowel or screw through the center for an axis. As they continued to work, they created more variations, some using combinations of plates or plates and bowls mounted on an axis. This was a rich environment with an interesting problem and materials. The children were given about an hour and a half to work on it.

This and other environments we have worked with produced a good deal of activity that, after a time, settled into some rather stable patterns. The teachers moved through the room, stopping occasionally with a question, a comment, or an intervention.

One teacher, Kathleen, noticed that all of the children were mounting the top halfway up the axis. This bias toward making things symmetrical had an unintended result: The pointed sticks—which were the best axis—happened to be longer than the flat-bottomed screws. Because children like things to be symmetrical, they mounted the tops halfway up the axis. Because the stick was longer than the screw, this meant that tops made with the sticks were farther from the floor and, therefore, less stable than when they were mounted on the screw. The instability led the children to discard that axis.

Kathleen was watching the children discard an axis that she knew would work better. She noticed that the children's insistence on placing the top halfway up the stick was keeping them from seeing the potential of the longer stick. She asked to borrow one of the tops with the discarded stick. The child, Monica, said, "Oh, sure, it doesn't work anyway."

Without speaking, Kathleen pushed the plate down on the axis until it was about an inch from the floor and then spun it. As it continued to spin much longer than any of the others had, the child turned and watched. She immediately lowered her other tops, as did most of the other children in the room, even though not a word was spoken.

This kind of intervention is supportive of the assimilation/accommodation process. Being able to see or hear how other people have approached a problem also supports the process. I once conducted an informal study in which we observed families interacting in the learning lab when it was open to the public. We repeatedly observed the way children made use of other people's ideas. We saw children looking around the room when they seemed stuck or had run out of ideas.

One boy was working on building a high tower from rectangular wooden blocks. When it reached a height of about 2 feet it fell down. This happened repeatedly, and finally the boy seemed to give up and walked away. He walked around the room watching people working on other kinds of problems. Suddenly he seemed to see something that gave him an idea, and he quickly came back and began to build again. As he did, he centered the blocks more carefully and built a 4-foot tower, which seemed to be as high as he wanted. It did not fall.

On another occasion, we brought classes into the lab to spend one to three weeks working with us. After the children found a way to do something, such as build a car that will go a long way, they seemed to enjoy hearing about other student's solutions. Often the children would go back and improve their cars based on ideas they had heard from other children, but seldom did they just copy what the other children had done. Similarly, the videotapes of Constance Kamii's work with children inventing arithmetic show that the explanations children give for how they solved a problem result in some of the children finding a way to do things that they think is better than the one they had before.

Re-Equilibration

Assimilation and accommodation are components of a process of understanding. Progress in understanding does not mean progress in the *amount* of content acquired. Progress in understanding means change in the way the content is *organized* and *coordinated*. Small accommodations in an existing way of thinking lead eventually to gaps and contradictions. When accommodation becomes impossible, because of these gaps and contradictions, the way of thinking becomes "disequilibrated" or "destructured." It breaks down. The process of restoring equilibrium is what Piaget called *re-equilibration.*

Garcia (1992) describes this process as follows:

> Re-equilibration resulted from constructing new structures, new coordinations, new operations, which accommodate without conflict the same contents that acted as perturbations leading to the disruption of the former structure. (p. 31)

A breakdown leads to the construction of new ways of thinking to accommodate the same contents that acted as disturbances leading to the disruption of the former structure. The new structure is more complex than the previous one. The process of re-equilibration leads to the construction of new structures with new possibilities and broader, more complex relations. This construction is not motivated by a need to acquire knowledge but, rather, by an internal need for coherence. In the process of restoring equilibrium, a better knowledge structure is obtained, but the person is not acting to do that. The person is acting to maintain internal relationships.

In the case of the conservation of liquid, Bobby's initial way of thinking might have included something like, "Taller means more" and "Water doesn't change just because it is poured from one container to another." Another idea might be, "The way to tell if something has more is to look." The idea that taller means more and things are as they appear is challenged by the idea that pouring water from one container to another doesn't change it. That idea challenges the perceptual reality only if it occurs to the person as having some relevance to the current situation. When it does, conflict ensues.

The conflict can be resolved by denying one part of the contradiction (decide one of the measuring cups had more liquid to start with), denying that a contradiction exists (it happened by magic), or using a different criterion for the decision. When a child changes the *way of making the decision,* he or she acquires a new mental tool that can be used in other situations. In Bobby's case, when he poured the water back into the measuring cups, he convinced himself that in this case logic was a better guide than appearance. As he is faced with that kind of conflict again, he might be more likely to trust his logic.

Students often experience this phenomenon when studying for an exam, especially an essay exam. As they study, they begin to see that information that seemed like disconnected bits could be ordered in a meaningful way. A former student of mine, now a kindergarten teacher, described it as "a lightbulb coming on." Once they find this order, the information becomes more meaningful and, thus, easier to remember.

We tend to think of children's knowledge in terms of what they are missing or where they are wrong. Piaget suggests a different approach.

He believes that children's thoughts, rather than moving from "wrong" to "right," should be viewed as growing from less to more sophisticated or complex. When confronted by a novel problem, we make sense of it as best we can. If we have opportunities to continue to solve problems of this type, our ideas might develop.

In the chocolate-bar problem described earlier, some children cannot get past the way the bars look. Piaget calls this "perception-bound." They make their bar exactly like the original, ignoring the requirement to make it with a different-sized end. Other children know that if it is built with a smaller end, the bar has to be longer, but they are not exact about it. They just add on until "it looks right." If we think these children are wrong, we will try to get them to see the "right" way. Usually this results in children learning what to say without really changing what they think. In Piaget's view, each child is in the process of moving from qualitative to quantitative thought, on a continuum of increasing exactitude.

When teaching is concerned with the construction of mental operations, it is a more complex and difficult endeavor than it once seemed. To "show" and "tell" children is not sufficient. We can't directly transmit the mental operations that are necessary. Even hands-on approaches are not sufficient, because the "minds-on" is what matters the most.

I once heard an audiotape of a classroom in which the teacher was trying to help children understand condensation. She showed them a glass of ice water. As condensation formed on the outside of the glass, she asked them where the water came from. The children said it came from inside the glass—a typical response.

Trying to "show" them, the teacher covered the top of the glass with cellophane and put a rubber band around it. The children then said the liquid went through the glass by seeping through tiny holes in the glass. The teacher put an empty glass in the freezer until it was cold, then had the children watch the condensation form. The children said that little bits of water had left tiny holes in the glass.

Finally the teacher resorted to her old method of leading children to the answer. Her voice changed, rising at the end of each statement in a questioning manner. The children responded in unison in a kind of sing-song rhythm. I doubt if any of them changed their mind.

Structures

 s children learn to perform certain kinds of operations, they grow into the realization that some of these operations can be coordinated. Piaget called these coordinated systems (such as seriation and classification) "structures." When completed, structures allow children to deduce new consequences that they had not considered previously.

Piaget's (1977) study of the construction of *seriation* is a good example. Children were given some metal rods of graduated lengths and asked to arrange the rods in order of increasing length. Preschool-aged children made two sets: big ones and little ones. By about age 6, children can seriate the rods, but they do so by some form of trial and error, often comparing each stick to every other stick to find the smallest one of each remaining set of sticks. By about 9 years of age, the child looks for the smallest rod in the set, puts it down, then looks for the smallest remaining rod, and so on.

In Piaget's study, after each child constructed the series, he or she was asked how many sticks were larger than the smallest one. The children counted the sticks and answered "six," the correct answer. Next the psychologist covered all of the sticks except the largest one and asked how many sticks were smaller than that one. The child who constructed the series by trial and error tried to look under the cover and finally said he

couldn't figure it out because he "can't see." The 9-year-old answered correctly. The structure of a series allowed her to deduce that if six sticks are larger than the smallest one, six are *necessarily* smaller than the largest one. This feeling of necessity is one of the indicators of a structure; the child has a sense that it must be this way, that it is obvious (Piaget, 1987).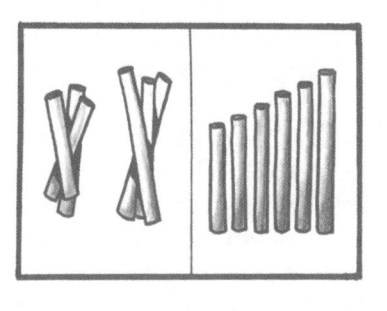

A structure is a coherent set of mental operations that can be applied to various contents. Piaget thinks that there are a very few general structures that are applied to all things or beliefs in a person's mental world. When these structures change, the result is a succession of complete reorganizations. During the period when a structure is changing, all new structures are possible, but only a few of them will work and those are the ones that tend to develop. In Piaget's view, operations become the "structured groups that give to thought its flexibility, its versatility, its ability to deal with novelty, its creativity" (Gruber & Vonèche, 1995, p. xxxv).

At some point, the structure is completed, and it is a tool that can be used throughout life. The organization of integers is one such structure. Once we know this sequence of numbers and operations that can be performed on them, we can use this idea, and we can integrate it into more complex systems of numbers. As adults, we do not have to give any thought to the relationships between the integers; we just use them.

Understanding the difference between a structure and a fact or an idea is important. A structure is an integrated system, an intellectual tool that can be used in a variety of situations. Knowing how to recite the numerals in order does not mean that a child understands numbers. Recognizing and saying numerals is a language problem. Understanding integers means understanding the *relationships* among the integers.

A structure allows me to make inferences that must necessarily be true. For example, because I understand the relationships among the integers, if you tell me that some number X is larger than 4, I also know that X is larger than 3 and 2 and 1. I can figure out these relationships even if I have not thought about them before because I understand how the structure works. Understanding the structure also means that a person can think *about* the structure, relate it to other structures, and perform operations on it. If a person does not understand the structure, he or she cannot do these things.

For example, because I know the structure of the integers, I can learn to perform operations on them, such as addition and subtraction. If I do not understand the structure of the integers, I can learn the procedure to follow in performing those operations, but I have no way of knowing, for example, that 4 can be made by $3 + 1$ or $2 + 2$ or $4 + 0$.

Piaget (Gruber & Vonèche, 1995) tells the story of his friend, an accomplished mathematician, who as a child was playing with stones on the beach. One day he arranged the stones in a line and counted them. There were 10. Then he arranged them in a circle and counted them. Again there were 10. He continued to do that until he convinced himself that 10 was independent of the way the stones were arranged. The idea of 10 was not in the stones, the sand, or the boy. It could not be seen, smelled, touched, or heard. The idea of ten-ness *emerged* in his mind as he acted upon the stones.

In classrooms, teachers try too often to give the idea of ten-ness to children or, worse, to assume that only mathematically inclined children can understand and to simply ask the others to memorize it. I would much prefer that children have a few ideas they understand well than many ideas they are able to remember but not understand. This is especially true in mathematics, which is so interrelated that children are seriously handicapped by early teaching that substitutes remembering for understanding. This is why the National Council of Teachers of Mathematics (NCTM) has adopted standards based, in part, on the principle of "less is more."

Understanding—An Inside Job

Understanding cannot be coerced. We may be able to make people act in certain ways, but we cannot make anyone—not even ourselves—

understand. The best we can do is make ourselves remember, and even that is severely limited. Alternatively, we can cooperate with the natural organic processes of learning by creating what Bob Witte of the Exxon Education Foundation called "capacity-creating conditions." We can create conditions that cultivate and nurture learning.

Intellectual growth is an organic process like growing a carrot from a seed. We do not assume that just because we can't predict, control, or direct the growth of the carrot, we should just wait for the carrot to reseed itself and grow new carrots. We try to create optimal conditions that nurture the growth of carrots. Likewise, we can create conditions that make it more likely that children will construct ideas, see relationships, think, and make sense of things. We can create these conditions if we give up the notion that we must control what and when children think.

Understanding Relationships

Bateson (1991) says that all information is "news of difference" (p. 188). Human nature is to detect difference—Bateson says that we create boundaries and divisions so we can organize information into meaningful sequences. For example, to a native English speaker, someone speaking rapid English still seems to be saying distinct words. To a person learning English, though, the same speaker seems to be saying a jumble of sounds. The learner hasn't developed enough of an understanding of the pattern to separate the sounds into words. When I was a kid growing up among native Spanish speakers, one of the first phrases I learned was *"mas despacio"*—more slowly.

The unconscious calculations that result in our perceptions rely heavily on comparison. The outer parts of the retina of the eye are sensitive to motion and change. What we see is difference. Our sense that a sound is coming from a certain direction is a result of a rapid and unconscious computation of the difference between the time of arrival of the sound at one ear and time of arrival at the other ear. We pick up information about differences, and we unconsciously construct perceptions from that information. We take the differences that we are able to detect and, from them and the ideas and knowledge we have already, we "create 'objects' and endow them with characteristics" (Bateson, 1991, p. 190).

We are not aware we are doing this, so we often describe relationships as if they were characteristics of objects rather than relationships among objects. Difference and relationship are the bases of understanding, and they are constructed as a result of comparisons.

> Where is the difference between this paper and that desk top? Obviously not in the paper; obviously not in the wood. It certainly is

not in the space between them, and it is a little hard to say that it is in your senses *and* my senses. (Bateson, 1991, pp. 152–153)

Difference is not a physical thing. It is relational. It is not *in* the object or the person; it emerges as a result of comparing the objects, in this case the paper and the desk.

The tendency to substitute objects for relationships has been especially devastating in the study of mathematics. In our culture, we seem to accept the notion that many of us will not be good at math. Comedian Paula Poundstone once said, "My body rejects math." She got a good laugh. If she had said, "My body rejects reading," she surely wouldn't have elicited laughter. Our lack of understanding of the nature of relational thought has led us to teach mathematics, in elementary school especially, as a series of procedures and operations rather than as relationships and patterns.

When my colleague Kathleen Martin asks a group of adults she works with about the Pythagorean theorem, most vaguely recall hearing about it and might remember that this theorem has something to do with triangles. Eventually someone comes up with the formula, $a^2 = b^2 + c^2$. Only a few people have any idea what the square means except that it calls for the operation of multiplying "a" by itself, "b" by itself, and "c" by itself. Kathleen then constructs a triangle out of little pieces of plastic and constructs a square on two of the sides. She shows the group that the areas of these two squares can be moved and reconfigured to make a square on the hypotenuse that contains the same area.

This is the difference between remembering a formula that indicates operations to be performed and understanding the relationships that led to the formula in the first place. A formula is a statement of relationships and regularities that someone in the past found. In school, most of us memorized formulas mindlessly and used them to indicate a procedure to follow. No wonder our bodies reject math!

A high school teacher, Vida, was teaching about the "golden ratio." The golden ratio is a ratio of 1.6, but most adults I have asked do not remember what that means. She showed them slides of rectangles and had them choose the one they liked best. Then she tallied the results and had them determine the ratio between two adjacent sides of the rectangle by dividing the smaller measure into the larger (e.g., 10 inches into 16 inches). Even though the rectangles were different sizes, the ratio of the ones that were selected was a golden ratio.

Vida told the class about the person who discovered this and that it is the relationship that most of us find most pleasant. She had the students measure each other and determine the ratio of body parts, such as the length of the finger to the length of the finger to the first knuckle. She created a context for the students to think about the golden ratio as a statement about how humans are constructed and what we like, rather than as a definition that has to be memorized. I haven't forgotten the golden ratio, and my guess is that her students haven't either.

In my classroom, I tried to give my students a similar opportunity to experience combinational reasoning. Combinational reasoning is used to solve problems in which elements can be put together in different configurations. I asked my students to solve the following problem (which I learned about at the annual meeting of the Exxon Education Foundation's K–3 Math Specialists project): Given 6 snap cubes with 3 red and 3 blue, how many different towers can be constructed? In this case a tower is defined as 3 cubes snapped together with the "chimney" on top. When you solve it for the 3-block tower, solve it for a 4- and 5-block tower (beginning with 8 and 10 cubes, respectively). Now, how many 6-block towers could you build with 12 cubes?

Some students tried to solve it by building a tower, taking it apart, and building another. Most developed a system of some kind. Some worked qualitatively, drawing the towers or writing symbols to represent the colors. A few expressed their results in a chart, allowing them to see relationships between the towers. One student created a formula to express the relationships. Each student used combinational reasoning at some level. If we were to continue to work on problems like that, the students would have a basis for understanding concepts such as factorials, combinations, and permutations.

Many helpful books have been written illustrating alternative ways to create environments in which children learn mathematics as a result of their own actions. Constance Kamii, professor at the University of Alabama, has published books and videotapes illustrating environments in which children "re-invent" arithmetic through their own actions, thoughts, and conversations. These are welcome alternatives to memorizing formulas and mindlessly following algorithms.

Preparing for Insight

In my Educational Psychology class, I asked the students to write detailed descriptions of a learning experience. All of them wrote about the struggle, the frustrating feeling, that someone else could see something that they could not see. Learning is a lonely thing at times, because we get a clear sense that even the most willing, benevolent, and skilled teacher cannot give us what he or she knows. The students also talked about the incredible feeling of relief, joy, pride, and excitement that came when they had learned.

Kenosha wrote about learning to tell time. She said that she knew people were seeing something when they looked at a clock and that whatever they saw allowed them to say the time, but she could not see what they were seeing. She described staring at what seemed like meaningless marks on the clock face. One day she asked her mother the time and looked at the clock. A minute later she asked again, and then again and again. She saw a relationship between the numbers her mother said and the pattern on the clock. She was very excited that she saw the key to the puzzle and was now able to tell time.

We all have had experiences of seemingly sudden flashes of insight. Often we make the mistake of thinking that we could have had the insight earlier, or that a specific explanation accounts for the fact that we understand it this time but did not understand it previously. I think that is a mistake. We focus so much on the moment of insight that we forget that an important part of insight is a prepared mind.

Although change and insight are sudden, they do not come without preparation and foundation. I attended a concert by a singer who, after working for 20 years in obscure nightclubs, had recently been "discovered" and had become a big star. At the end of the concert, she said it had taken her 20 years to become an "overnight success."

As teachers know, the process of preparing for insight does not guarantee that the insight will come, but insight probably won't occur without preparation either. What we think of as sudden insight is a result of organizing relationships in such a way that the insight emerges. This is a difficult concept because once we have constructed the organization, it doesn't seem like something we have constructed; it seems like it is simply there. It is like those puzzles that at first seem like unconnected pieces of wood glued to a background but suddenly they spell "peace." Once we have seen the word, the puzzle doesn't go back to looking like unrelated pieces of wood again. We have learned how to see it differently.

Ideas such as "larger than" are relational. The notion that *this* stick is longer than *that* stick does not reside in one stick or the other, but it may emerge when I hold the two sticks next to one another. Initially this is a difficult idea for most of us because once we are accustomed to using relational ideas, we are not aware that they are relational and we think it is *in* the sticks.

In response to a question from the audience at the Association for Constructivist Teaching Conference, Constance Kamii asked someone to show her "two-ness." Someone held up two pieces of paper. As Constance questioned the person, it became clear that two-ness is not in the two pieces of paper unless you already hold the idea. We invest the papers with that relationship after we already know about it.

In the classroom, inventing a way to order things is more important than being *shown* order. Instead of being told about a taxonomy of leaves or insects that someone else discovered, what if children are allowed to examine groups of specimens and think about how *they* would order them? They could argue for why they think a certain way seems best to them and also listen to their classmates argue similarly for their way of doing it. Then, when they find out the way scientists have agreed to order the taxonomy, it would be more interesting and make more sense.

Piaget's Stages

The kinds of reorganization that occur in the lives of children have some patterns. Piaget called these patterns "stages." Piaget (1977) identified four stages, characterized by significant changes in the way a child is able to relate to his or her world: sensorimotor, pre-operational, concrete operational, and formal operational.

1. In the *sensorimotor stage* (ages 0 to approximately 18 months) children relate to the world through their senses and actions. Babies' tendency to put everything in their mouths is one way by which they investigate objects through the senses—in this case, the sense of taste and touch.

2. In the *preoperational stage* (ages 2 to 7), children are developing symbolic processes, such as language. According to Gallagher and Reid (1981), Piaget emphasized the importance of correspondences, which develop in this period and are the beginning of under-standing transformations.

3. By school age (7 to 11 years), children are in the *concrete opera-tional stage*, having the ability to apply operations to the manipu-lation of objects.

4. The child in the *formal operational stage* (12 years to adult) is able to think logically and to hypothesize.

Referring back to Piaget's seriation experiments, we observe the stages at work: young children sort the sticks into piles of "big" and "little." When asked how many are bigger than the smallest, they cannot answer without looking, even though the children have correctly answered the question, "How many are smaller than the largest?" Older children and adults can arrange the sticks in a series and, having answered the question, "How many are bigger than the smallest?" they think it is silly for you to ask how many are smaller than the biggest. It is obvious to them.

This brief overview does not do justice to the complex ideas in Piaget's notion of stages. Considerable controversy exists about Piaget's stages, and some evidence suggests that they may more appropriately be considered trends than stages. They are dynamic moments in an unfolding process and very much a reflection of a child's experiences.

Usefulness to Teachers

Piaget's studies of the development of children's thought are most helpful when viewed as the development of a frame of reference. As a teacher, I want to know the child's frame of reference so I can better understand how he or she is likely thinking about things.

No matter the age of the person, when I see a child reasoning about a problem qualitatively, I know that it may be a necessary early stage in being able to move later to a quantitative understanding. The child might know that a chocolate bar with a 2 × 2 end has to be longer to have the same amount of chocolate as a bar with a 3 × 3 end. But at this stage the child might not have a way to figure out precisely *how much* longer, even though he or she has a more sophisticated understanding than the child who simply builds the bar the same length as the one with the 3 × 3 end.

This use of Piaget's work on stages is much better than trying to use the stages as a diagnostic tool or an indicator of how children are progressing through the stages. As Eleanor Duckworth (1996) says in her book, *The Having of Wonderful Ideas*, learning to *be* Piaget is more important than learning *about* him.

One of the best ways to learn to see children as Piaget did and begin to understand what he was trying to describe with his stages is to *do* what he did. A colleague of mine who grew up in Geneva, Switzerland, says that he remembers seeing Piaget on his bicycle, white hair streaming from beneath his beret. My colleague remembers him because whenever Piaget saw children, he would stop and watch them. One way to grow in understanding children is to watch and listen carefully when you are around them.

Another, more formal way to understand children is to repeat some of Piaget's and Inhelder's experiments. Do them with several children of various ages. The conservation of liquid experiment is a good one to do with preschool children. The conservation of volume experiment, as modified by Duckworth, is good for elementary school children. The seriation experiment works well with children in preschool through middle school and can be used to see the difference in thinking in a range of ages. A good experiment for older children is the pendulum experiment.

In the pendulum experiment, Inhelder and Piaget (1958) presented children with a pendulum in the form of an object tied onto the end of a string. The students were given the means to change the length of the string, the weight of the object, the amplitude of the swing, and the force of the push. The problem they were given was to find out what affects the frequency of the pendulum swings.

Older children (above about age 12) and adults may be able to think about this problem using what Piaget called "formal operations." According to Inhelder and Piaget, the formal operational person knows how to produce *combinations*, in which one factor varies while the others stay constant (e.g., the older child may use a single length of string, the same amount of push and amplitude, but with various weights). However, in the earliest form of formal operational thinking the person does not produce these combinations systematically.

Experiment *Experience*

With a middle school or high school student (or an adult), present a pendulum in the form of an object tied on the end of a string. Give the student several lengths of string and objects of different weights. Allow him or her to push the object with different forces, or start it from different heights if the child wishes. The challenge is to figure out what affects the frequency of the pendulum swings.

How does this child go about solving the problem? Do you see evidence of "formal" thought? Is the child able to imagine the pendulum swing without having to actually swing it? Is the child able to vary a single factor while holding all others constant? Is the child able to exclude factors that play no role in the solution to this problem?

The succession of frames of references that Piaget described as stages represent progressive detachment from an individual frame of reference to a commonly held, invariant one. This invariance is what allows the person in the pendulum experiment to construct a system of possible inferences. It is what allows a child in the seriation experiment to know that if there are six objects smaller than the largest one, there have to be six larger than the smallest one.

The increasing distinction between self and world reflected in Piaget's stages leads to the ability to reflect on one's own intellectual processes, to think about thinking, which gives us a new command over our thought and growth. Earlier stages are not discarded or "grown out of." Instead, a later stage is opened up and made possible by attaining the earlier stage. That is why, though the ages at which children develop these new abilities are different, the *order* in which they develop is believed to be constant and universal.

In their book *Psychogenesis and the History of Science*, Piaget and Garcia (1989) discuss the many instances in the history of science when evidence was available to change theories long before these theories changed. They suggest that the change could not have occurred until the current structure of thinking changed. As Gruber and Vonèche (1995) suggest, given that humankind does not change in the light of such evidence, "to credit the child with a facile empiricism, readily fitting thought to experience" (p. xxxvii) seems a bit odd.

Piaget's many studies show, in every case, that children begin far from adult ways of thinking about things and must grow into these adult views. Piaget suggests, with ample evidence, that they grow into these views the same way that adults historically did so; they have to re-invent them through their own activity. In *Psychogenesis and the History of Science*, Piaget and Garcia (1989) discuss how adults who discovered new ideas had to engage certain kinds of problems and, through their own actions on these problems, construct the new ideas. Piaget suggests that children must do the same thing:

> The main fruit of genetic epistemology is this discovery that the only way in which we get knowledge is through continual construction, and that we can have no enduring knowledge without actively maintaining this process. Something else, therefore, will surely be constructed, something that still lies ahead, that will replace whatever the naive realist chooses to canonize today. And so on ad infinitum. (Gruber & Vonèche, 1995, pp. xxiv–xxv)

Piaget and Garcia (1989) argue that the Greek scientist and philosopher Aristotle and children alike are limited by what Piaget and Garcia call "pseudo-necessity." Pseudo-necessity arises from, among other things, the notion that whatever exists does so necessarily. "There is a sense that 'it has to be that way,' which imposes strict limitations on what can be accepted as being possible" (p. 58).

Pseudo-necessity led Aristotle to associate all motion with a goal related to the form or structure of the thing moved, like a kind of internal motor. Children share this view.

> Very young children, for example, may believe that the wind is produced by trees (which sway by themselves), by waves that rise, or by clouds, which spontaneously move ahead. (Piaget & Garcia, 1989, pp. 67–68)

Uneven Development

One of Piaget's ideas that is important to teachers is what he called "horizontal decalage"—each child develops unevenly (Gruber & Vonèche, 1995, p. xxvii). This is demonstrated in his famous studies of conservation. As discussed earlier, conservation describes the understanding that an object can change form (as in pouring liquid from a measuring cup into a beaker) without losing substance. The example cited earlier of pouring liquids into containers of different sizes was one of Piaget's conservation (of liquids) experiments. Conservation clearly is an important idea.

Piaget found that children understand the conservation of liquid before they understand conservation of area. A child knows that the liquid in the two different kinds of containers *has* to be the same because "all you did was pour it from one container to another." That same child is given two rectangles made of small squares and told that this is grass for a cow to eat. Initially the rectangles are the same size and shape. The child says that both cows have the same amount to eat. When the squares in one rectangle are spread out so they have space between them while the other rectangle is left in its original form, the child does not think they are the same any more. In Piaget's terms, the child conserves liquid but does not conserve area. These ideas develop separately.

This notion seems odd to many adults, but if we think about our own development, it is not odd at all. When someone wants to know how old I am, I am tempted to ask, "In what respect?" In some areas I am old beyond my years, and in others I am immature. My knowledge is well developed in some areas and naïve in others. Therefore, I am not surprised that this is true of children.

It also is true that individuals develop at different rates, so knowing what *some* or *even most* children do is not always helpful in predicting what a given child will do. The fact that a child has developed a set of operations that allows him or her to discover an idea such as conservation of matter does not mean that the child will discover it without being presented a problem whose solution requires him or her to think in this way.

To help this to happen, teachers might carefully design environments that promote children's thinking in various ways. Some situations would require grouping, some analysis, and so forth. Many teachers and parents are not equipped to construct or evaluate learning environments in that way. An alternative is to construct environments in which children are engaged in actively figuring things out, solving problems, building things, and collaborating with one another. If these environments present problems that are close enough to real life to be complex and are meaningful to children, the children will develop these intellectual tools.

One of the most important things we do for children is to develop their minds. We have not only created material tools such as shovels and computers, but we also have developed intellectual tools by which to furnish children's minds. Although we are well intentioned, the problem is that, unlike the shovel, we cannot give children an intellectual tool and show them how to use it. What we have to do is to create the conditions under which the child is able to construct the tool. This requires a different kind of sensitivity, and it is one of the most neglected aspects of Piaget's work. As Gruber and Vonèche (1995) put it:

> [F]or Piaget the growth of the intellect, rather than something that happens to the child from the outside, is a process of self-construction, governed by existing formations of cognitive structures. To be sure, it happens in relation to the world, and it is a process that has evolved in such fashion that its results are biologically and socially adaptive; the world plays its regulative function. But it is not a matter of stimulus and response, push and pull. Rather, environmental events are assimilated as well as they can be to existing structures, chewed over and digested, and, finally, only occasionally do they result in fundamental changes in such structures. (p. xxx)

Co-Evolution

Most of us have a sense of Charles Darwin's theory, even if we don't know much about the details. One of his ideas that has influenced us is that evolution progresses from simple to complex. The first time you saw a newborn baby, were you surprised that all of the details were present? I remember being fascinated by those little lines on the baby's palm and knuckles. It seemed to me as if the baby shouldn't be finished in such exact detail. I had absorbed the Darwinian notion that things begin simple and grow to be complex. Chaos scientists and current evolutionary theorists challenge this notion. For example, Stuart Kauffman (1995) says: "Life emerged, I suggest, not simple, but complex and whole, and has remained complex and whole ever since" (pp. 47–48).

We cannot see a child's mind the way we see the lines on his or her palm. Many of us act as if we think children's minds are simple, like a palm with no lines, and the mind becomes more complex with time. We act as if we think the complexity results from the addition of information in a linear, logical, accretion process. We think of children's thought as "primitive" in the same sense that we consider the thought of ancient peoples to have been primitive.

We are wrong on both counts. Children think in complex ways, as did ancient peoples, but their thought is different. The *basis* for thought is different, and it occurs in a different context. Ideas such as this about the way children's thought develops have influenced the way we talk to children, the kind of toys and tools we make available to them, and the way we organize their school experiences.

Jane, a first-grade teacher, reported an incident that we refer to as "closet talk." Jose and Keeta, children in her class, came into the supply closet one day. Jane was there getting some materials but had not turned on the light, so the children did not know she was there. As the children talked to one another, Jane was amazed at the level of their conversation. It was far above what she heard in the classroom.

Another teacher, Robert, was doing one of Piaget's early experiments in which Robert told a story to a child, Nancy. Robert left the room, and another child, Julio, came in. Nancy told the story to Julio. Nancy left, Robert came back, and Julio told the story to Robert. A video camera was running continuously in the room where the story was being told. Robert, the teacher, was amazed at the sophistication of the children's conversation when they were in the room alone. As a result of these experiences, both of these teachers changed the way in which they speak to children.

When applied to curriculum, the idea of simple to complex leads to the idea that children must "master" certain ideas before they can be introduced to other, more difficult ideas. People assume, for example, that children must understand addition before they can learn multiplication. Teachers have reported that, in reality, some children understood addition for the first time while they were learning multiplication. Ideas are not building blocks. They are dynamic, alive, coalescent.

In Piaget's descriptions of the patterns of development in children's thinking, children clearly think in complex ways and form complex ideas. Many of these ideas parallel the forms of thought common in earlier times (Beth & Piaget, 1966; Piaget & Garcia, 1989). What develops is not the complexity but, rather, the basis for their thought. We use the ideas we have to think about anything new that comes along. Occasionally the framework for these ideas, the foundational ideas, undergo a transformation and reorganization. The result is not only that we have different ideas but also that we have different ways of thinking or we think on a different basis. This is what develops over time. Children change because they have a new basis for their thought, not because their thought is simple.

I suggest that we need to try to understand how children's thought makes sense to them in their context, in terms of the other ways they are thinking and making sense of things. This approach retains and honors the complexity of children's thought.

My friend Helen was bringing her 3-year-old daughter Hillary to see me. Helen lived in Illinois, and I lived in Arizona. Every time Helen mentioned the trip, Hillary asked, "How are we going to get there?" Helen answered, "On an airplane." That didn't seem to satisfy Hillary. The next time an airplane flew overhead, Helen pointed to it and said, "We're going on an airplane." Again Hillary was not satisfied and asked again, "How are we going to get there?" She finally added, "Are we going to have to climb on top of a tall building?" Only then did Helen realize that Hillary had never seen an airplane on the ground.

Summary

Memory is an important part of learning. It is especially important in the sense of extended memory, in which written documents and electronic documents have created almost limitless storage of records. Learning to organize and access this "extended memory" has become very important in recent times.

Understanding has become more important than remembering. One of our most important tasks as adults is to help future generations develop their understanding and their ability to think and imagine. To do this, we must appreciate the reality that children think differently than adults do. Children's thought is not simpler; it is different. It has a different basis. Piaget described this as a series of stages that children go through sequentially in their development.

Understanding these stages allows us to "get inside a child's head" and have some insight into how children are thinking. That is crucial if we are to help children develop their minds so each child will be able to make his or her own unique contribution to the world.

> The true direction of the development of thinking is not from the individual to the social but from the social to the individual.
>
> —LEV VYGOTSKY

6

The Social Aspect of Ideas

Jean Piaget helped us to understand that concepts emerge from children's reflections on the results of their actions. He also knew that we do not think, learn, understand, and act alone. We are part of a culture. We use languages and other symbols to think with, we interact with other people, and our thoughts are formed partially in response to these interactions.

Russian researcher Lev Vygotsky focused primarily on language, culture, and social interaction as they support and assist children's intellectual development. His objective was "to explore how human society provided instruments to empower the individual mind" (Bruner, 1983, p. 137). Vygotsky published little, and what he did publish was not available until the late 1950s and not available in English until after 1960. He died of tuberculosis in his 30s.

Many researchers, including Vygotsky himself, have focused on the differences and disagreements between Piaget and Vygotsky. The delayed availability of Vygotsky's work and his early death limited exchanges between him and Piaget, making the extent of their disagreement impossible to determine. Their clear areas of difference, however, do not negate the ways in which certain parts of the theories are compatible. These areas are precisely those that are important for teachers and parents.

Bruner (1983) says,

> The world is a quiet place for Piaget's growing child. He is virtually alone in it, a world of objects that he must array in space, time, and causal relationships. (p. 138)

Bruner contrasts this with Vygotsky's world, which was

> an utterly different place, almost a world of a great Russian novel or play. . . . [G]rowing up in it is full of achieving consciousness and voluntary control, of taking over the forms and tools of culture and then learning how to use them appropriately. (p. 139)

In brief, then, Piaget helps us to understand the way a child's thought develops in her or his own mind; Vygotsky helps us to understand how to help children use the work of those who have gone before them.

The Relationship Between Spontaneous and Academic Thought

Many of us have had a sense that at least some of our academic preparation has nothing to do with everyday life. A chasm seems to divide our everyday lived experience from the academic knowledge in texts and school. Students typically complain, "Why do I have to take trigonometry? I'll never use it!"

Vygotsky understood that experience is of two different kinds, and sometimes the two are so different that they seem almost unrelated. He called one of these basic forms of experience *nauchnyi*, which frequently is translated as "scientific." According to Wertsch (1996), it also could be translated as "academic" or "scholarly," reflecting the fact that Vygotsky saw scientific concepts (*nauchnye ponyatiya*) as being tied to the discourse of formal instruction (p. 27). Vygotsky differentiated this academic knowledge from what he referred to as "spontaneous" or "everyday" knowledge.

Vygotsky (1986) focused on the way children learn academic concepts, which "originate in the highly structured and specialized activity of classroom instruction and impose on a child logically defined concepts" (p. xxxiii). Although teaching is concerned primarily with developing these academic concepts, Vygotsky holds that this teaching has to be rooted in common experiences and understanding. Good teaching can be thought of as a process of building bridges between everyday knowledge and academic knowledge.

Vygotsky initially believed that scientific thought is more evolved than spontaneous thought. Later, he held that the two kinds of thought have *different* purposes, rather than greater or lesser purposes. In the Modern era, and still today, certain kinds of knowledge—particularly scientific knowledge—are still privileged and are considered "better" than others. But our culture also has stereotypes of people who are so academic that they can't function well in their everyday lives.

We do not want to replace spontaneous concepts with academic ones. I know that when I appear to be standing still, I am actually swaying within a small range governed by sensors in my leg muscles. But I do not act that way or think that way in everyday life. In everyday life I am standing still.

What is needed is an understanding of academic concepts and the way they relate to spontaneous concepts. Too often, we try to help children understand academic ideas without relating them to the ideas they already have constructed from reflections on their own experience. When children have tried to see patterns for themselves or find a way to organize a collection, for example, they are more likely to benefit from seeing how adults go about organizing things or the patterns that adults see.

When introducing a new topic, a simple way to begin is to find out what the students already know about the topic and what they would like to know. Brenda, a kindergarten teacher, did that once before beginning a unit on insects. Amazed at the children's answers, she wrote what they said on large sheets of paper and posted them in the room. She then created environments for children to find answers to their questions. She said they ended up learning much more than she had originally intended to teach.

As another simple way to begin, for example, instead of telling children a definition of "mammal," give them a list of things that are and are not mammals and see if the children can figure out what the rule for classification is.

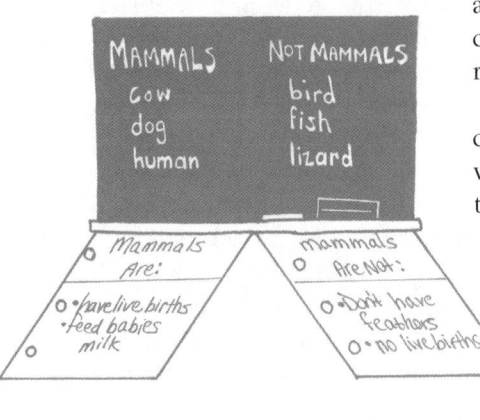

Schools or parents who have computers might ask children to write using the computer and then use spelling and grammar checkers to correct their work. In time, these checkers will have taught the children a great deal about spelling and grammar.

Knowing More than We Can Say

When we are trying to explain something to another person, we might reach a point when we struggle to find the right words. We might say, "It's like . . . " and the other person might say, "Oh yes, I know what you mean." Sometimes the person *does* know, but often it isn't quite what we meant. If the message is important enough, we try again to find different words, or to think of an experience or story that will relay the message more clearly.

This is a common, everyday experience. We have something in mind that helps us to determine whether people have understood us. We know when someone is saying something that is not "it," even though we cannot say, and do not know, explicitly what "it" is.

Theorists generally agree—and most of us know from experience—that we know more than we can say. We sense that knowledge is somehow in our bodies or in some part of our mind that is not conscious. When someone asks, "How did you do that?" we have to stop and think and sometimes make several attempts before we can explain what we just did. Piaget noticed that children begin life in tune with the physical world, both in their own bodies and in the concrete objects around them. He suggested that we understand first with our bodies and only later can think about and describe what we know.

When trying to teach someone else a skill, I often find that I do more showing than telling. When I taught swimming, I would move my arms and turn my head as I tried to help the new swimmer learn to breathe. I haven't been able to describe it well in words. My hands and arms just seem to know how to do it. Doing something and talking about it are two very different things.

Reconstructing What We Know

Both Piaget and Vygotsky believed that knowledge is not simply expressed in language or transferred from unconsciousness to consciousness. It is *reconstructed* in symbols. Language and other symbol systems are a *different* way to know. Vygotsky and Bateson wrote about the differences between the world as we perceive it and the world as we think about it in language. What we see, for example, is a whole and integrated picture. As I look out my window, I see an entire scene, all at once. I do not move from left to right seeing a leaf, branch, space, grass, sky, and so on. Speech, on the other hand, occurs linearly, one word at a time. The process of describing in speech what I see out my window is necessarily a reconstruction.

Piaget (1976) discusses how 4-year-olds talk about walking on all fours. They describe their actions as "one hand, then the other one, then one foot, then the other one" (p. 2). Piaget noted that this is a fairly universal way by which children describe that action. In reconstructing the pattern, they describe their movements in the simplest way rather than the most accurate way.

Use of Symbols Creates Possibilities

The process of reconstruction is different for adults than it is for children. For experienced adults, using language is a matter of selecting a symbol that best matches their sense of what they want to say. For an inexperienced child, using language is a matter of learning and manipulating the symbols. One of the great achievements of childhood is learning to use language and other symbols. Vygotsky argues that the use of language changes thought, enriching and clarifying it. This is the case for written, as well as spoken, language.

Younger children need help in learning the symbols as the adult community uses them. Vygotsky believes that this process occurs as adults interpret children's actions. It is a loop: A child acts; an adult reads into the child's actions, figures out the help the child needs, and provides it. This leads the child to read something into her or his own action that was not there initially, and eventually the child uses the action or word intentionally for that purpose.

What we think of as a mental symbol is, on a neural level, a pattern of activation of neurons. Siegel (1999) says that such a pattern "contains information, and it creates an effect." The effect is the development of "some fundamental building blocks of internal experience" (p. 162). As we go about helping children build a brain, we may want to think about how the organization of the brain reflects the kinds of problems children can solve and can learn to solve.

Siegel (1999) says that "evolutionary pressures have required that the brain become specialized in its problem solving skills. We inherit the genetically pre-programmed capacity for information processing of a particular sort" (p. 163). The brain is currently considered to be made up of modules, each of which is specialized for handling specific kinds of information in specific ways. One type of memory, according to Siegel, handles information about objects and events; another handles information about time and space. The two together allowed us to find food and remember where enemies might be hiding, he suggests. Other, more complex systems allow us to transform this particular kind of information into generalizations, which allow us to more efficiently use our mind by creating adaptations that are useful when events are similar enough to require the same or similar strategies. As the modules of the brain interact to create the experience we call thinking, learning, and adaptation, they also contribute to the future capacity of the brain to solve problems.

Our current understanding of brain functioning implies that the mind determines the kind of problems we are able to solve; more important for education, the kind of problems we have an opportunity to solve contributes to the kind of brain we will have in the future. I want students to solve problems through a process of forming ideas from what they know, trying those ideas, noticing what happens, and changing their ideas. Because I think this is an essential and adaptive process, I teach by creating problem-solving situations for children, by responding to situations they create from a problem-solving perspective, and by helping students to develop ways of dealing with problems that in turn give them the skills and confidence to attempt to solve broad ranges of problems. If I thought that the essential skill for human life was the ability to remember large amounts of information, I would approach teaching differently.

Vygotsky (1986, p. xxvii) discusses the way a child uses adults to help him or her learn. For example, a child learning to indicate something with gestures at first makes an unsuccessful grasping movement directed at an object. (Vygotsky used the term "gesture-in-itself" to designate this stage of the development of gesture.) When the mother comes to the aid of the child, the situation acquires a different character. "Gesture-in-itself" becomes "gesture-for-others." Others (mother, in our case) interpret the child's grasping movement as an indicatory gesture, thereby turning it into a socially meaningful communicative act.

Only afterward does the child become aware of the communicative power of his or her movement. The child then starts addressing the gesture to adults, rather than to an object, which was the focus of his or her interest in the first place. The child is the last person who consciously comprehends the meaning of his or her own gesture. Only at this later stage does a gesture become "gesture-for-oneself."

A child is in the company of others, constantly, and these other, older people interact with and interpret the child's actions and language. People assume a meaning that the child does not initially intend. As a result, the child's action takes on new possibilities. At some point, the child *intends* this new meaning.

Gregory Bateson (1972) talks about meta-communication, which is the premise that language is used to communicate within and about a relationship. According to Bateson, a cat's meow is the same whether the cat wants water or food or to be let outside. This same meow works because what the cat is doing is invoking a caregiving relationship. In a sense, "meow" means, "Mother, come take care of me," or something like that.

Vygotsky suggests that from similar beginnings, which the adult interprets as meaningful, the child begins to learn adult ways of interacting and speaking. This social interaction is not *transferred from* the mother to the child. The child does not somehow take it up. The child reconstructs it in the context of an interpersonal relationship.

Symbols Cannot Substitute for Reflection on Experience

When children learn to speak, they speak according to their newly developing ideas about how language works. My colleague Dr. Cecilia Silva told me that research on language development shows that English-speaking children say things such as "I losted it," even though they do not hear adults say "losted." Children speak based on their current understanding of language, not just in imitation of what they hear.

Vygotsky noted that children cannot learn some concepts by being told about them even if they understand the words being used. Vygotsky argued that academic concepts cannot be transferred in "ready-made form" (1986, p. xxxiv). The teacher and the students have to have the same experience, the same symbols, and the same understanding of what they mean. This understanding does not come about through formal word definition. It comes about through the ability to refer one's experience or thought "to some known class or group of phenomena" (Vygotsky, 1986, p. 7).

Gregory Bateson (1987) says:

> I can write words on the blackboard and wipe them out. When wiped out, the writing is lost in an entropy of chalk dust. The ideas are something else, but they were never "on" the blackboard in the first place. (p. 57)

Analogies, metaphors, and stories evoke more of the details of the experience. The message seems to be in the words because we can read or hear something and think, "That's it!" as if the words *carried* the message. Most often (maybe always), the words give us a description, a way to talk about what we know already. If two people do not share an experience in common, the words have no meaning. This is one of the reasons that two people can listen to the same lecture or the same sermon and hear something completely different. What we hear is not in the words; it is in the relationship between the words and our experience. If we do not have the experience to be able to hear, the words fall on deaf ears.

When someone tells us a story, even though the details of the experience are different from ours, a certain resonance between the experiences allows us to identify the experiences as similar. The story creates a bridge between our experiences.

Siegel (1999, p. 62) says that narrative creates "shareable stories," "determines patterns of behavior," and "may influence our internal lives (in the form of dreams, imagery, sensations, and states of mind)." Siegel points out that stories are a quintessential social event. Stories are co-constructed in a social context and include "the essential features of social interaction and discourse. The teller produces verbal and non-verbal signals that are received by the listener, and then similar forms of communication are sent back to the teller." This process, which Siegel compares to an intricate dance, "requires that both persons have the complex capacity to read social signals, to share the concept of the existence of a subjective experience of mind, and to agree to participate in culturally accepted rules of discourse."

Humans are fundamentally social beings, and stories are arguably our most natural form of interaction within a social context. They are a powerful conceptual tool for teaching and learning. Stories can also serve as input to more analytical processes that identify themes and connect them to other themes identified by scholars who generate publicly held knowledge. Stories can connect us to one another and to the larger stories collectively held by our culture as content knowledge.

Conditions That Help Children's Reconstruction

That children can do more than they can say means that we must not rely exclusively on children's verbal responses as an indicator of their understanding. We have to create environments in which we can see what children are thinking by watching what they are able to do and how they do it, as well as by what they say about it.

Children need help in reconstructing their knowledge on a verbal plane. One of the difficulties here is to help the child *reconstruct* knowledge rather than *abandon* his or her implicit knowledge and memorize or repeat words.

> Rather than simply modeling, the adult teacher must create first a level of "intersubjectivity" (Wertsch, 1996), where the child redefines the problem situation in terms of the adult perspective. Once the child shares the adult's goals and definition of the problem situation, the adult must gradually and increasingly transfer task responsibility to the child. (Diaz, Neal, & Amaya-Williams, 1992)

In the volume (chocolate bar) problem described earlier, my task is to help the child understand the problem as I understand it. My responsibility is to observe the child and see whether he or she understands what "end" means, for example, as that is crucial to understanding the problem. I am not supposed to solve the problem for the child but, instead, to help him or her understand the parameters of the problem. Typically, a child makes a bar exactly like the model, but with the first set of blocks like the new end, thereby creating something like the one illustrated in Chapter 4.

To the extent that this is not disruptive, we should encourage children to work with one another, to consult with one another, and to discuss the results of their work with one another. This is especially helpful when children are able to talk with other children who are at different points in their understanding. Although the age segregation in schools makes this more difficult, many teachers have overcome this difficulty by creating relationships with other classrooms of older or younger children.

We can learn a lot about how children are thinking by listening to the way they talk to themselves and to each other. Instead of teaching children to give correct responses, which masks the current state of their thought, we can listen to them for information that will help us know what kind of problem we should present to them or what kind of environment we should construct to help them develop their thought.

In our work with third graders, we noticed that they did not understand two-dimensional to three-dimensional transformations. My colleague Kathleen created an environment with a number of games and tasks involving transformations. In one task, she asked the children to hold an object between a light and a screen, creating a two-dimensional shadow of a three-dimensional object.

They also played a game in which one child constructs a simple figure out of snap cubes; draws a picture of the top, front, and side of the figure on a piece of graph paper; puts the figure in a bag; and attaches the drawing to the outside. This child then trades bags with another child who has done the same thing. The children try to reconstruct the figure in the bag from the drawing on the outside of the bag. At the end of a week of playing in these and other similar environments, the children had developed a much more sophisticated understanding of the relationship between two-dimensional and three-dimensional representations.

We also can help children through their interaction with us. When we provide language in response to children's need for it instead of in advance of their need, children associate the symbols with their common experience, just as the child learned to gesture in Vygotsky's example.

Brenda, who was teaching kindergarten science, began by asking the children what they *know* about plants and what they *want to know* about them. From those two lists, she brought in books and various materials and tools that the children used to pursue the answers to their questions. Their study of plants led them to wonder about the insects that were eating the plants.

The day I visited the class, I was impressed by the sophistication of the children's language. These children had all been held back because they were believed to be "delayed." Yet, here they were, a few months into the year, discussing an insect's abdomen and thorax. Brenda did not teach them this vocabulary directly. She simply used those words in referring to the things in the room and answering their questions.

The Evolution of Ideas

I deas are spontaneous, disorderly, alive, self-organizing, and self-renewing. Ideas evolve. What I think today is not what I thought yesterday. I remember when I was in the fourth grade and fell in love. I also remember that in the eighth grade I fell in love again and laughed at what I thought was love in the fourth grade. In some ways, my life could be characterized as a series of times when I thought I was obviously wrong before but now I knew truth.

Ideas and understanding evolve. Not only do my ideas evolve individually, but also as a culture and a people. In the same way that a child constructs his or her own intellectual life, we as a group construct and live in a culture, and this culture changes, sometimes quickly and sometimes more slowly. At any given time, though, it appears to us to be "how things really are." Piaget demonstrated that children see what they are able to see. It is as if they are wearing a pair of glasses that colors what they can see.

The difference, for children and for the culture, is not in the quantity of information but, rather, in the way the information is organized and the ways it is constrained by underlying beliefs. For example, Piaget and Garcia (1989) describe how young children's belief in the primacy of horizontal and vertical movements causes them to describe incorrectly the trajectory of a tiddlywinks:

> When playing a game of tiddlywinks—(pressing one's finger on the edge of a token lying on a carpet, thus causing it to leap into a high-sided box), children can obviously see the curved path taken by the token, but they interpret it as follows: The token slides horizontally across the table, and when it arrives near the box, it jumps up vertically to pass over the wall of the box. (p. 79)

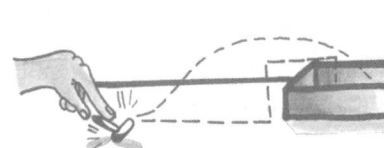

Cultures are similarly limited by commonly accepted underlying beliefs. At any point in its history, a people can see only what their current understanding allows them to see, not what is actually there.

Language allows us to use symbols to stand for objects and conditions and to experiment on these rather than experimenting on the real thing. Piaget believed that these "thought experiments" confer an evolutionary advantage. Language and thought allow ideas to evolve. Without them, innovations occur genetically, and when an organism is based on an innovation that is not workable, it has to die. With language and the ability to think in terms of hypotheses or "what-if," we gain the ability to allow an idea to die while we remain alive.

Like Piaget, Vygotsky believed that we are not limited to our *biological* nature. We create a specifically *human* nature as we develop cultures. The key to this development is the development of symbol systems such as language. The use of symbols *creates* new meaning.

Marti (1996) discusses cross-cultural studies of mathematics. In these studies, cultures that have not developed symbols for representing mathematical ideas have developed "forms of counting that follow certain mathematical principles" (p. 73). Marti notes, though, that these cultures do not develop mathematics beyond counting. The symbol system for counting seems to open the door to the development of more complex mathematical concepts. The very act of being able to symbolize something enables us to think about it in a different way.

Bruner (1990) discusses the way that human culture allows us to go beyond the constraints of our biological nature:

> We were slow to grasp fully what the emergence of culture meant for human adaptation and for human functioning. It was not just the increased size and power of the human brain, not just bipedalism and its freeing of the hands. These were merely morphological steps in evolution that would not have mattered save for the concurrent emergence of shared symbolic systems, of traditionalized ways of living and working together—in short, of human culture. (p. 11)

Learning to think with a new symbol system gives a child a tool rather than simply a new set of facts. The child has to receive opportunities to become thoroughly familiar with the tool so it becomes something to think with and not just a procedure to follow. Children who have a new tool play with it instinctively. In our study of good teachers, we found that one way good veteran teachers know if a child knows something is by the way the child plays with the idea (Martin & Reynolds, 1993).

Playing with Ideas

Vygotsky believed that, in play, children act beyond their current understanding. Laura Berk (1994) notes that although Vygotsky did not write much about play, he did accord it "a prominent place in his theory. He granted it the status of a leading factor in development" (p. 31). Stuart Brown (1995), a psychiatrist who studied the effects of the absence of play and in the lives of people convicted of violent acts, observed that play is common to all warm-blooded animals that feel safe. Although play sometimes is viewed as frivolous, it is anything but that. Brown notes that play is intense, engaging, and, on many occasions, dangerous. Children skateboarding or doing wheelies on their bicycles are cases in point. Brown points out that this is not just fun; it is fun at the edge of danger.

Play is also spontaneous. Among those who have studied children and animals at play are Brian Sutton-Smith, Jane Goodall, and Fred Donaldson. These scholars conclude that play is a fundamental learning mechanism. Goodall (1995) says:

> Play teaches young animals what they can and cannot do at a time when they are relatively free from the survival pressures of adult life—

when they are dependent on their mothers to take care of their needs. Thus, they have time to explore, to test, and to learn about the world around them. (p. 17)

Play is a way for children to imitate and learn about the adult world. It also is the way the species develops new ways of doing things. Stuart Brown (1995) calls play "a fundamental organizer, like a whirlpool in a flowing stream" (p. 9). It is the way that a species achieves flexibility and innovation. When a person is not immediately concerned with survival, he or she is free to play with materials, actions, and people. Even at mortal risk, play is essential to our survival and our continued development.

How do we create the conditions that will help children play with ideas? Brown (1995) identified two conditions as important for play: (a) feeling safe, and (b) being well fed. He also characterizes play as spontaneous: If the goal supersedes the intrinsic joy of the activity, it ceases to be "pure" play (p. 8). Imposing a goal other than the activity itself can turn play into what Dewey (1980) calls "drudgery."

Feeling Safe and Well Fed

Abraham Maslow argued that people are born with basic needs including "physiological hungers"—needs for safety, belongingness or love, and self-esteem (Hoffman, 1988, p. 154). Maslow noted that once "physiological needs are relatively well gratified," there then emerges a new set of needs, which we may categorize roughly as the safety needs. Once physiological and safety needs are satisfied, needs for "love and affection and belongingness" emerge. Then the whole cycle "will repeat itself with this new center" (Maslow, 1970, pp. 38–42). Thus, people who are hungry think only of food, and people who are afraid for their safety are preoccupied with trying to protect themselves. If children are to learn, they must be well fed and feel safe. This feeling of safety includes feeling safe physically—from intruders, bullies, and the like.

Schools and neighborhoods have to ensure that children are physically safe in school. Today, children who are exposed to news of school shootings and other such violence may need reassurance unlike that required previously. Safety measures, both physical and psychological, probably have to be more sophisticated than in past years. A teacher's responsibility, in addition to cooperating with these initiatives, is to create an atmosphere in which all people are respected. This means we do not ignore slights, slurs, insults, or bullying but, instead, help children to understand and appreciate the value of all people and the danger of prejudice.

Name-calling is not a harmless childhood game. We must help children to understand that name-calling is a first step toward violence, because violence begins with depersonalizing and dehumanizing people.

Many schools and communities have established breakfast and lunch programs to feed hungry children. Teachers can further assist children to avoid physical discomfort by allowing reasonable breaks so children can get a drink of water and use the restroom.

Feeling Intellectually Safe

Feeling safe intellectually means that students believe they can say what they really think and be reasonably sure that people are listening. It means that, though other students might disagree, even loudly and emotionally, the disagreement will be about the idea and not a personal attack or a show of power. It means that we care about one another and value each other's talents and perspectives. In this sort of classroom, students can play with ideas and try out different things.

Feeling safe intellectually also means that students have reason to believe that the teacher recognizes their competence and does not try to make the student unnecessarily dependent. The teacher does not ignore or dismiss a child's idea. Furthermore, the teacher does not assume that a student needs help until the student shows evidence of that need. To give only the help needed is difficult for a teacher. We observed in the learning lab over a long period to see how adults try to help children and the effects of this help. We found that most adults gave children much more information than they needed or used. Children, on the other hand, helped each other by showing one another how to fix the problem that was immediately blocking them. Often that was all that the child needed.

On one occasion in the lab, a child was trying to cut a paper cup in such a way that it could stay in the air a long time when it was suspended over a vertical column of air produced by a fan blowing through PVC pipes. The child had cut slits in the top to make a kind of fringe. The cup would stay up only a short time. The child handed the cup to another child, who took the cup, bent the fringe down, and handed it back. The cup stayed up longer. Not a word was spoken. As I watched, the first child constructed several other kinds of flying cups, all of which had some version of bent flaps.

After the cups had all been used, another child got an old, intact cup that had been wadded up and thrown away. She straightened it out and cut some flaps around the top edge. It didn't fly very well.

The teacher came by, and the child showed him that the cup didn't work very well. Without thinking about it very much, the teacher said, "The flaps are cut the wrong way." He then launched into an explanation. The child thanked him politely and waited for him to leave. Then she tried to straighten the cup some more where it had been crushed. She said quietly, "I think it's because the cup is all wrinkled." She was right.

A class was assigned to construct a car that would travel the farthest distance down a ramp and across the floor. The materials available were a rectangular wooden block, four axles, wheels of various sizes with rubber tires, and rubber bands of various lengths and widths. As I watched the children racing their cars, one child's car was swerving as it came down the ramp. It started off going farther than the others, but it did not end up as far because part of its distance was curved. The same thing was happening with several other cars, and none of the children seemed to notice. Take a moment to think about what you might do in this situation.

Nel Noddings (1992), a professor of education at Stanford University, has written about the importance of caring in schools. She visited the university where I teach. In conversation with the faculty, she asked us to think about the teachers who had an impact on us and our learning.

Noddings suggested that it was not their method that we remember, or how much they knew, but, instead, that they cared about us. That is true for me. I don't remember anything particularly remarkable about the way those teachers taught. I do remember the few teachers I had who seemed to like me. They had a great impact on my life and on my future. We learn better and are more productive, then, when we feel that people care about us.

In a study conducted in a factory years ago, the experimenter studied the level of light on the factory floor and decided that productivity would increase by increasing the light. Lights were installed and, as predicted, productivity increased. Several months later, more lights were installed, and productivity increased again. A third time lights were installed, with the same effect. A few months later, the researchers removed some of the lights, and productivity still increased. They surmised that productivity was not related to lighting at all—it increased because the workers thought management cared about them.

Playful Classroom Environments

If children are well fed and safe, they will play. With young children, creating a playful environment is mostly a matter of providing them with interesting objects with which to play. The problem in dealing with young children is not how to get them to play but, instead, to think about the ways we unnecessarily curb or constrain play. I have seen kindergarten teachers create wonderful centers and then ring a bell every 10 minutes and have the children rotate to a new center. After a short time, these centers reveal little playfulness.

Older children and adults tend to play more with ideas and symbols. Although we still engage in some play with objects as we move toward adulthood, much of our play is with words and other symbols. We converse, debate, and verbally interact in other social forums.

Public Scrutiny of Ideas

Once new ideas have begun to take shape, they develop into concepts, which are exposed to public scrutiny. This invites the expression of other views and allows people to offer counterevidence, to point out "holes" in an argument, and to offer more reasonable interpretations.

Bruner (1990) argues that public discourse is what holds our culture together. Children have to develop the ability to engage in discourse. "We live publicly by public meanings and by shared procedures of interpretation and negotiation" (p. 13).

Trying to ensure that children get the "right answer" is much less important than encouraging them to make good arguments, listen and respond to others, and grow in their thinking as a result.

Constance Kamii, a professor at the University of Alabama, has used this kind of public discourse as a way to help children test their invented arithmetic. The teacher poses a problem on the board, such as

$$11$$
$$+9$$

The children decide what they think the answer is and the teacher lists all of the answers on the board. Then the children argue for their answer by explaining their logic. For this problem, one child might say she thinks the answer is 20 because she took 1 away from the 11, making it a 10. She knows that $9 + 1$ is 10, so she added the two 10s together, and that made 20. The other children say "agree" or "disagree." In Kamii's video of such a classroom, one child said, after listening to the others' explanations, "Now I disagree with myself."

In my own class of older students, I ask them to answer a question in writing, and then I begin the discussion by asking for as many *different* ways to answer the question as we can find. This tends to keep the discussion more open and playful and allows more facets of the issue to surface.

Zone of Proximal Development

Sometimes a teacher can try to teach you something, and you just don't get it. Later, someone else can say the exact same thing and suddenly it makes sense to you. When I am the teacher in that situation, it is frustrating, especially when the student raves about some explanation I have given repeatedly and someone else gets the credit.

We tend to think this is because the other person found the "right way" to explain it, and if we had tried that way earlier, we would have been able to learn it then. This notion is a leftover of the Modern assumption that we are empty vessels to be filled. What happens in those instances is actually a readiness that allows the teaching to be effective.

In the same sense that we know more than we are able to say, Vygotsky says we learn to do things unconsciously and spontaneously before we are able to control these functions. The process of representing thought in words or other symbols makes our thoughts more precise and more useful to us. In a similar way, the ability to use a function or skill intentionally is important.

Vygotsky wanted to determine what enables a child to gain this control. He says it is the "child's capacity to use hints, to take advantage of others' helping him organize his thought processes until he can do so on his own" (Bruner, 1983, p. 140). In a sense, adults and more competent children can help children function beyond their ability and, in doing so, children pull themselves up to the next rung of the ladder.

This is not the same thing as direct teaching. Just telling or showing the child how to do or think does not work in Vygotsky's world any better than it does in Piaget's. The child's ability to take advantage of adult help depends in part on where the child is in his or her thinking and the nature of the adult help.

A child's current thought occurs within a kind of envelope of possibilities that he or she is able to understand at a given time. A child just learning to add, for example, might be able to think of 3 + 3 as three disks in one pile and three disks in another pile moved together to make a pile of six. The child might then be able to follow an adult who shows him or her that this is the same as a pile of one disk moved together with a pile of five disks to make a pile of six disks. The child, however, might not be able to think that the problem "3 + 3" is related to the problem "4 + 2." The envelope in which a child can think with adult help is what Vygotsky called "the zone of proximal development." We now use the acronym ZO-PED.

If teachers and parents are to help children, our help has to stay close to the child's thought. As in martial arts,

> you don't try to stop your opponent, you let him come at you—and then give him a tap in just the right direction as he rushes by. The idea is to observe, to act courageously, and to pick your timing extremely well. (Waldrop, 1992, p. 331)

What is a "tap in just the right direction"? Sometimes it is showing someone the next move when he or she is stuck. It may consist of a word or a phrase. Once we were doing a version of Piaget's volume experiment. A child was presented with a piece of paper having a drawing of two rectangles of different sizes representing islands in a lake. On one of the "islands" was a "house" erected from blocks, and the child was asked to use small blocks to construct a "house" on the other one that would have just as much room. The child was to build on the whole island but not off it (not in the water). In this version of the experiment, we had several papers with different-sized "islands," so when the child finished one, he or she was asked to do another.

As I observed a boy working on the first volume problem, I noticed that he behaved much like the children whom Piaget reported in his volume experiments. The boy built his building the same height as the teacher's building and then compared the two buildings by moving his hand across the top of them. He declared that they had the same amount of room. When the teacher asked the boy if he was sure, he said he thought they were the same but he wasn't absolutely sure. The teacher asked him how he could know for sure that they were the same.

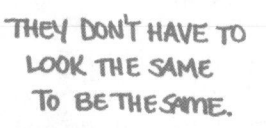

The boy reconfigured his building so it looked like the other one and then added to it until it looked exactly the same. This caused him to build beyond the island. The teacher said, "but yours is in the water." He took the part that was in the water and put it on top. He looked puzzled. The teacher said, "They don't have to look the same to be the same." He repeated that to himself, and his eyes lit up. He repeated it again. Then he constructed buildings successfully on the rest of the papers (with different rectangles). After each one, he said, "They don't have to look the same to be the same."

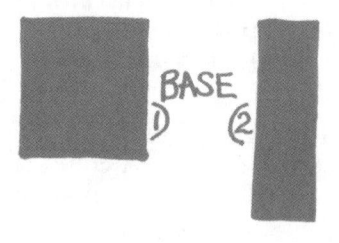

Sometimes a tap in the right direction helps a child to create limits. When children approach new problems or new materials, they do so in an exploratory way, starting with their current constructions. Sometimes they get lost in exploration. They act as if they are immobilized by the many possibilities. They do not have to be "freed" from a limitation. They need assistance in thinking about the problem in a way that constrains it so it is more manageable.

For example, we asked children to construct a "diabolical cube" (a 3 × 3 × 3 cube) from a set of preconstructed pieces. Many of the children did not think about the whole cube and the necessary coordination of the pieces to build it. Instead, they thought only of the next piece to add to their current construction. They did not seem to notice that a 3 × 3 × 3 cube could not be constructed if one of the sides was already larger than three cubes in any direction.

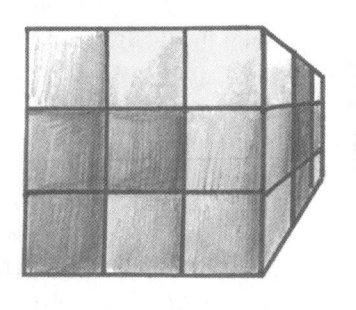

My colleague, Kathleen, went to the table to sit with some children who were building the first wall longer than three cubes. She began making her own cube and intentionally made it longer than three cubes. She made comments to herself such as, "That won't work. It's already larger than three cubes. I won't be able to make the cube if one part is already bigger than three cubes."

Some of the children did not change what they were doing. Others seemed to understand, for the first time, that each side would have to have a necessary constraint if they were to build a 3 × 3 × 3 cube. Kathleen had no intention of "making the children see" this point but, rather, imparted a subtle suggestion of an important feature in constructing the cube.

That only some of the children responded indicates that the teacher's help was within the ZO-PED of some, but not all, of them. When adults go beyond a child's ZO-PED, it does not affect them unless we try to coerce them into abandoning their way of thinking for ours.

Sometimes the best help comes from a peer who has figured it out. My students report that another student who is slightly ahead of them in the same class often helps them. One of the reasons could be that the other student's help is still within the struggling student's ZO-PED.

A classroom encompasses many different ZO-PEDS. If we try to teach in a standardized way so all children progress through the same material at the same rate, some children will be bored and others will find that what we are doing is unintelligible. If we want children to adopt adult ways of doing things, we have to find ways to allow them to work together and help one another, as well as work with the adults in the room. When we create environments for children, we also must free ourselves to observe children, assess where they are and what they need, and interact with them.

Summary

Although each of us has to construct our own knowledge, we do not have to do this alone. Each generation does not have to reinvent the wheel. In the past, we did not understand that knowing something and being able to describe it or tell someone else how to do it are different. Because of this misunderstanding, we have overemphasized verbal responses and penalized children who know in other ways.

We now understand that knowing and reconstructing knowledge in symbols are two different processes. We also understand that symbols cannot substitute for experiences. We cannot bestow knowledge on another person. Nevertheless, we can help children to find ways to symbolically reconstruct their knowledge. To do that, though, we must have experiences in common with them.

Playing with objects and ideas is an important part of developing intellectually. Teachers have to create the conditions that allow children to be playful. We also must help children to share ideas with one another. Children need to learn to participate in culturally accepted forums for public knowledge, including subjecting their ideas to public scrutiny.

Teaching is not just about leading children. It also is about effectively following them. To teach someone, I have to know how he or she is currently thinking about something. I have to be able to act within the person's zone of proximal development.

7

Teachers act as if
teaching causes
learning when actually
learning should be an
occasion for teaching.

—KATHLEEN MARTIN

Learning as a
Condition for Teaching

I n the physical world, a force acting on an object can cause the object to do something. The intellectual world has no such equivalent. Intellectual life is about meaning, description, implication, juxtaposition, insight, and the like.

This does not mean that we have to let kids discover meaning on their own. What it means is that instead of looking at causes as one does in a physical model, we need to think about conditions and constraints, as one does when dealing with living things. It also means that teaching does not and cannot *cause* learning. Thought is adaptive and responsive to environments. It is dynamic, unfolding, transitional.

For many years we thought that students learned what we told or showed them. We organized the curriculum around a "point," concept, or idea that we wanted students to learn. We now know that students learn from the entire environment. In a lesson designed to teach geometric shapes, for example, children might learn to label shapes correctly, at the same time learn what geometry is and what mathematics is—even what learning is about.

This phenomenon is what Gregory Bateson (1972) calls "deutero-learning" or "learning to learn." In a given environment, we are learning about that environment, and we also are learning about environments of that type. Knowing that, we must think about *how* kids are interacting with the environment, not just *what* they are supposed to be learning.

Malcolm Gladwell (2002) described a study by John Darley and Daniel Batson at Princeton University. They met individually with a group of seminarians from Princeton Theological Seminary. The students were asked to complete a questionnaire about why they decided to study theology. They asked each seminarian "to prepare a short, extemporaneous talk on a given biblical theme, then walk over to a nearby building to present it" (p. 164). One group had been asked to speak on "the relevance of the professional clergy to the religious vocation." Others were given the parable of the good Samaritan, a biblical story about a man who had been beaten and left for dead by the side of the road. In the story, a priest and a Levite walk by but do not help. The only man to help was a Samaritan, a "member of a despised minority."

Half of the members of each group were told they needed to hurry because they were already late for their talk. Half of the members were told that they had plenty of time but might as well start walking over. On the way to the talk, each seminarian "ran into a man slumped in an alley, head down, eyes closed, coughing and groaning. The question was, who would stop and help?"

Surprisingly, neither the reason they were at the seminary nor the fact that they had heard the parable of the good Samaritan predicted who would stop. The students who stopped were the ones who had been told they had plenty of time but might as well start walking over to the nearby building.

Context, as shown in the experiment, is powerful. Even small things in the environment that we might overlook can have important and unexpected results. Unfortunately, most of us too quickly look to an attribute of the person rather than to the context to explain what someone is doing. This is what psychologists call "Fundamental Attribution Error" (Gladwell, 2002, p. 160), which is the mistake of "overestimating the importance of fundamental character traits and underestimating the importance of situation and context." Gladwell cites a study in which a group of people watched videos of two groups of equally talented basketball players. The first group was shooting baskets in a poorly lit gym, the second in a well-lit gym. The first group missed a lot of shots. The observers rated the second group as superior basketball players compared with the first group, wrongly attributing the first group's poor performance to poor skill rather than poor lighting.

Gladwell (2002) reports another experiment in which a group of people were asked to play a quiz game. They were paired up, and members of each pair drew lots to see who would be the "questioner" and who would be the "contestant." The questioner was asked to make a "list of ten 'challenging but not impossible' questions based on areas of particular interest or expertise, so someone who is into Ukranian folk music might come up with a series of questions based on Ukranian folk music" (p. 161). The contestant attempted to answer the questions. Afterwards, both people were asked to estimate the general knowledge of the other. Gladwell says that the contestants rated the questioners as more knowledgeable.

Knowing that we are prone to these fundamental attribution errors, perhaps we can be cautious about the judgments we make about children. Knowing the importance of context, perhaps we can try to seek a broader understanding of the situation. For example, if a child is consistently late to school, before we decide that he or she is lazy or doesn't care, perhaps we should find out if the family owns an alarm clock.

Learning Is Self-Organizing

 second attribute of learning is that it is self-organizing. Important intellectual work is accomplished in the organizing of it.

In my class in child development, I spent time in my early days trying to organize the material in ways that would make it clear and obvious to the students. I took this to such an extreme that one semester I handed out complete sets of knowledge maps to the students. As I lectured from these, I looked into a sea of bored faces. I realized that the interesting, exciting, meaningful learning was going on in my office as I prepared for class. I was "giving" the students the *results* of the process. These preorganized materials were inert; they were the dead, lifeless leftovers of a dynamic process. The meaning is in the act of making sense of things, not in hearing the sense that someone else has made.

This does not mean that everyone has to "discover" things on their own all the time. An important way for us to see new possibilities is to hear how someone else views a situation or problem. Thinking through a problem with students can be helpful, but only if they are free to use this as a spark for their own thought rather than a model for what they *should* think. The subtle interconnection between us and our environment is such that "our most private thoughts and feelings arise out of a constant feedback and flow-through of the thoughts and feelings of others who have influenced us" (Briggs & Peat, 1989, p. 154).

Students might find formal concepts more understandable and useful if teachers link formal concepts to more "natural" ones that students encounter in their daily lives. Bruner (1983) says that

> ordinary, natural-kind concepts have meaning and utility and connotation. They lend themselves, for example, to caricature and stereotype. . . . They fit into narratives like a hand in a glove. (p. 119)

Vida Trevino, a high school teacher, began a lesson by telling students: "A German man did a study on who likes pictures the most. I thought we could see which pictures we like and see if we can figure out why." The teacher showed the students slides with a series of figures and had them vote on the ones they liked best in each set. The teacher then measured the "best" ones and found that what they had in common was the ratio of their sides: when students divided the short side of a figure into the long side, the resulting ratio was 1.6, which is described as the "golden ratio."

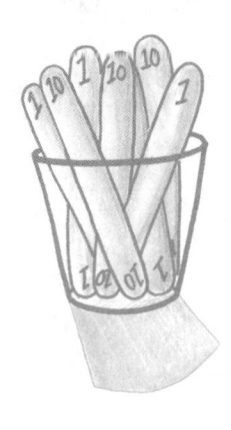

Kay, a kindergarten teacher, had a large clock. She would write on the board "10:15 recess" while saying "at ten-fifteen we will go to recess." Every now and then Kay looked at the clock and remarked about the time. She did this for various events, such as lunch. In this way, her students were learning to tell time in subtle ways.

Other teachers have a ceremony for beginning the day, such as adding sticks to a pile as a way to keep track of the number of days since school began. Some teachers trade in 10 plain sticks for one different kind of stick that stands for 10. As the students add the sticks each day, they count them together. These students are practicing counting and laying groundwork for understanding place value. These activities create fertile soil for learning to self-organize.

Thought Is Adaptive

The ability to think adaptively requires the ability to organize and communicate our ideas and act on them. It also requires that we hold ideas loosely and recognize that our understanding is always partial. Freedom consists in understanding that the ideas I hold today, while the best I have, will have to be replaced someday. As clear as things seem to me today, the clarity is the result of a construction, a best guess about how things are. This allows me to act.

If I understand that the clarity is merely an ordering, a way of thinking that is useful, perhaps I can use ideas without sinking them so deeply into my mind that I cannot reexamine them when I need to and will not have to defend them to my detriment. We need to wear our ideas as a "loose garment." For many of us, though, our ideas have become too much like second skin.

We do not have to do anything to move ourselves and the children we teach into this adaptive stance. As Kauffman (1995) says:

> Our intuitions about the requirements for order have, I contend, been wrong for millenia. We do not need careful construction; we do not require crafting. (p. 84)

Thought and understanding do not require careful construction. We do not understand solely as a result of someone showing us connections. We notice differences. We form relations between ideas, and as these relationships grow into complex webs, they undergo transformations.

Thought moves naturally through overly chaotic and overly rigid phases. When we first begin to think about something, we can feel these phases. The confusion and overwhelming sense that all of the details are equally important gives way at some point to an organizational scheme, a point of view, which usually feels like *the answer*. If it is a big enough idea, it sometimes seems to me that I spend time looking at most things through the idea so that no matter what you might say to me, it reminds me of this idea. At those times I am not teachable. I am not open to new viewpoints or ideas or information.

Thankfully, at some point I become open and begin to "move" again. Eventually I reach a place of mature understanding in which I can hold ideas rather loosely because I have a structure in place that allows me to do so.

The order that moves us out of chaos cannot be imposed or given to us. It is the ordering, not the order, that matters. It emerges. In an apparently vast region of possibilities, chaotic systems settle into relatively few patterns. This also is true of human thought. The possible ways of thinking are limited by human nature and the nature of the world. The world has settled into a relatively few of the infinitely possible patterns. We have evolved in this world, and we are uniquely well equipped to detect certain patterns and not others. As Whyte (1978) says, "As Montaigne believed, and biology confirms: [we are] one species, one set of basic structures and potentialities" (p. 4).

In an interview with Scott London, Margaret Wheatley (1996) talked about the experience of self-organization of knowledge. She said "Yes, to get into the messiness of data before you try to decide what it means. . . . You can't get there without going through this period of letting go and confusion" (p. 3). How often do we allow children to get into the "messiness" of something and experience the confusion, the letting go, and the exhilaration of constructing a way of thinking about it that makes sense to them? We can't do that always, and perhaps not even often, but sometimes children should have those experiences. As a matter of fact, we should make sure that we allow ourselves to have those experiences on occasion as well.

Some teachers fear that students will "just think anything" unless they are carefully guided. They won't. The possibilities are constrained by the understanding that we are all humans with experiences of a similar world.

One of the mistakes people have made is to assume that because thought is constructed, any thought is as good as another. Students who take this point of view argue that essay questions asking them to write what they think cannot be graded because all thoughts have equal value. Nonsense. Arguing that there is a *right answer* is different from arguing that some answers are more useful, complete, or sophisticated than others. Even young children can understand some of the ideas of calculus, but they do not understand them with the same precision and elaboration as do older students. A kindergarten-level understanding may be *correct*, and important, while still being simpler and less sophisticated than one would expect from a high school senior, for example.

Ideas Are Linked

nce we come to understand something, we are not the same as we were before. Not only do we have the new idea, but it also changes other, related ideas.

This concept is analogous to the way the blood gets from the feet back up to the lungs. When the muscle contracts, it squeezes the blood up the vein and through a little one-way valve. When the muscle relaxes, the flow of the blood downward closes the valve so the blood cannot flow back down the vein. The human mind acts as if it has those little valves in it. Once we know something, once we come to some new understanding, we cannot go back to the way we were before.

I remember when I first became aware that I was not a good listener. Until I knew that, I was able to dominate conversations. After I knew it, I was painfully aware of it and could not go back to my previous, somewhat comfortable ignorance.

Many of us think of evolution as if it occurs in a static universe. We think of only the organisms themselves evolving. Actually, organisms are linked to settings and to one another. As Kauffman says (quoted in Waldrop, 1992):

> If the frog evolves a longer tongue, for example, the fly has to learn how to make a faster getaway. If the fly evolves a chemical to make itself taste ghastly, the frog has to learn how to tolerate that taste. (p. 310)

Ideas are linked. They co-evolve. When humankind begins to walk up a higher peak in one area of life, it changes the nature of all the other peaks. Although this linking of ideas is important, the interconnection also can be limiting. If I choose to surround myself with people who are like me and who think like me, I might feel comfortably assured of knowing truth, but it is an illusion. It is like convincing myself that this is the highest peak by wearing a hat that blocks the view upward.

Kauffman says that the heart of self-organization is in what the chemists call *catalysis*, a process whereby a chemical speeds up a reaction between other chemicals. He says, "What I call a collectively autocatalytic system is one in which the molecules speed up the very reactions by which they themselves are formed" (Kauffman, 1995, p. 49).

A similar process is at work in thinking. A new idea affects a number of other ideas. Ideas link together like a web, and new ideas or ways of thinking move through the web. Teachers report, for example, that children often understand addition better after they learn multiplication. Similarly, when older students learn algebra, they gain a different understanding of arithmetic.

This is one of the problems with the curriculum developed during the scientific management period described in Chapter 1. The assumption was that ideas should be arranged and taught in a logical sequence, as if they are building blocks. The mind, however, operates in *psychological* connections, which frequently are not the same as logical or historical ones.

Defining Meaningful Knowledge

O f all the ideas that have evolved, which ones should be passed along to the next generation? How do we decide that? How do we decide what information children need, what ideas they should understand, what ways of thinking we should help them develop? Knowledge is useful or meaningful in a context and for a purpose. Some might argue that a certain general knowledge is important for all members of the community. At a time in history when less was known, we might have been able to argue that all knowledge is important, but that clearly is not possible or desirable today. Careful decisions have to be made not only about the ideas, skills, attitudes, and ways of thought that matter but also the level of detail at which they matter.

Decisions about the usefulness of some bit of knowledge cannot be made in isolation. Knowledge is contextual; it exists and is valuable in some context and in relation to some purpose. Questions about whether something is worth knowing are not answerable without knowing "for what purpose?" or "in what context?" Dr. Donna Mae Miller at the University of Arizona said of the fitness movement, "Fit for what purpose?" She pointed out that for hair stylists, sufficient strength and endurance to hold their arms in the air and stand on their feet for long periods might constitute fitness, whereas fitness would be something different for someone else.

I showed two film clips to my class one day. Both clips showed a narrator who had a seed, a seedling, and a limb from a maple tree. The narrator asked the question, "Where did the stuff in the limb come from? How did it go from this little seed to this big limb?" The fourth graders in the film clip said things like, "The sun goes in somehow and makes it," and, "It comes from the minerals in the soil."

In the second film clip, the narrator asked the same questions of a group of graduates on graduation day at Harvard. They used more sophisticated language but basically gave the same kinds of answers. No one said that the stuff in the limb is made of air, or long-chain carbon atoms. Later my class broke up into pairs to talk with one another about this and some other experiences. One man, Jack, called me over, obviously frustrated. Jack said, "I can't get Dennis to understand." I asked Jack what he was trying to get Dennis to understand. Jack said to Dennis, "You tell her." Dennis replied, "I just asked him why anyone needs to know about photosynthesis."

I thought that was a good question, and it is one that we may be paying more attention to. As educators, we may be getting better at assessing the relevance of knowledge. Although in many classrooms the teacher may move blindly ahead, sure that students need to know whatever is in the textbook being used for the class, on the whole we are seeking to recover meaning and relevance in our curriculum decisions.

Dr. Maxine Greene, a professor at Columbia Teachers College, suggested that the criteria for what people need to know is that which will help them live their lives. She pointed out that because I live in a world where AIDS is a very real threat, I need to understand enough about the immune system and viruses to understand what I read about this disease.

A biology professor at my university, Dr. Ray Drenner, became concerned about the gap between students' lives and the traditional biology class. He examined contemporary news magazines and clipped articles related to biology. He made these articles available to students and taught them the biology necessary to understand these issues. Students like his class, and they see biology as relevant and useful.

But we still have a long way to go. When we teach, we may go astray not only concerning the level of detail, we also may get hung up on avoiding ambiguity at all costs. We have a tendency in school to teach the least ambiguous member of a set.

Think about the tests given in elementary school. If you can answer by filling in the blank, choosing true or false, or selecting A, B, or C answers and the test can be graded unequivocally as right or wrong, this is unambiguous information. When taking this sort of test, I often want to qualify the question or answer by writing things in the margin, such as, "It depends. In situation x I think this is so, but not in situation y." This acknowledges that the context is more complex and ambiguous than the test question makes it appear.

Seldom, if ever, are students asked to find the limits of the ambiguity or to reason about context. Yet, this is the most important thing that you and I do in daily life. We seldom need to remember the exact answer or formula, but we often need to think about a similar situation, reason about what might apply here, try something, and observe the result.

We need to prepare children to estimate, figure things out, and reason together. We do that by providing environments in which our students are called upon to do that and by valuing the way children reason even when their answers are not the best. Valuing children's reasoning does not mean we have to abandon the idea that some answers are better than others, that some are more meaningful. It means that the answer alone is not important apart from the reasoning that produces it.

Creating Learning Environments

Although learning is too complex and dynamic to be managed or controlled, it can be nurtured and cultivated by creating conditions that allow it to grow. The teacher's job is to create environments for learning, to watch and listen and think about how students are interacting with and in these environments, and to respond to learning as it is occurring.

Conditions to be considered in designing learning environments include the physical environment (including materials and tools available for children to think *with* and the tasks and problems for children to think *about*) and interactions among the people in that environment.

Classroom Environment

People are embodied creatures. We live in bodies and in the world in a physical way. Yet, many of us experienced school as a denial of our bodies (except our eyes, ears, and, occasionally, mouth). We need to consider how children are invited to use their bodies in the environment. If students are investigating sound, for example, we might think about how we can help them feel the vibration in their chest bones in response to certain sounds, or to feel the way air vibrates in their throats when they sing.

What conditions have we created in classrooms that ask students to ignore or deny their bodies? I have seen rooms where children have to sit at uncomfortable wooden desks for hours at a time. In middle school and high school, I have seen students sitting at desks that are too small for them. In contrast are schools that have comfortable couches, areas on the floor with pillows, rockers, and the like (but usually not past third grade, for some reason). I have visited schools where students are allowed to get a drink of water only at specific times. They go out in a long line and wait to get a few swallows of water before the teacher asks them to move on so the next child can get a drink. Again, by contrast, I have visited schools where teachers have large containers of water and paper cups in the room and students are free to get a drink whenever they wish.

What does the physical environment of the classroom say to the student? When I visit a classroom, I try to notice how I feel in the room. Some rooms feel peaceful and invite movement, some create a sense of several different kinds of spaces, some feel sterile, some feel controlling. A few rooms I have visited seemed to invite change and to reconfigure in response to a need. In some schools, the entire classroom is open to public view, and other rooms have some nooks and crannies that allow students to find private spaces to be alone and to think. Most rooms I have visited, however, seemed static.

In some schools, the materials and books seem to belong to the teacher. The teacher gives the books to students or students ask for them or ask permission to get them. In other schools, the materials are in places that are readily accessible to students. One school has racks of books in the hallway, which students are free to borrow and return without a check-out system. A teacher visiting the school asked the principal if she wasn't concerned about students stealing the books. The principal replied that students often go into people's homes and public places without stealing things. She told me the school had not lost a single book.

The things displayed in a room and on the walls, I believe, make a statement about what is valued. If the room is decorated before the students arrive, the values reflected are those of the teacher. Some teachers spend the early days of the school year decorating the room as a community. These rooms reflect the life and history of this group of people, rather than just the teacher's accumulated materials.

Making the Community Part of the Classroom

John Dewey (1913) said that schooling should be only one means of education, that education happens throughout the community. What environments are in your community and how can they be used? I am not suggesting traditional field trips, which tend to be treated as a break from learning. I am suggesting that the community has places that can be used as learning environments. A park, a botanical garden, a museum—these can be great resources.

Though these places have the potential to be just another field trip they also have the potential to be learning environments. The difference is in how the teacher and parents work with the environment. When the children go to a museum, do they have to be in a line, reading the labels or listening to a guide? If they're going to an art museum, is it in the context of their own art or is it an isolated experience?

One of my teacher education students, Madonna Tully, created canvases of oil paints that children can touch. These paintings allow children to feel the effects they saw in canvases that hung in the museum, which they could not touch.

Another teacher's class studied the Impressionist period. The students went to the museum to see paintings and sculptures from that period. Then they created their own exhibit. They carefully matted their "impressionist" work and hung it in a "gallery." The class offered tours, complete with docents and security guards.

Sometimes the community can become involved in transforming environments in the school as well. One school worked with a local garden company to re-create a courtyard. An employee of the company worked with the kids, planning how to create a pleasant area that would attract birds and butterflies. The company also donated some materials, and the kids used the materials and knowledge to transform the courtyard.

The Container Store, a company specializing in better uses of space, helped a teacher rethink her classroom so it could be more versatile. Another store, Home Depot, helped us to create a "take-apart" area for children to disassemble discarded machines. The employees also came to help children learn how to use the tools.

Materials, Problems, Tasks

To adopt new materials and methods of teaching is not enough. We need to radically rethink materials, problems, and tasks. Many good curriculum materials are available today. What makes the difference is the way they are used. Instead of using materials to illustrate ideas, we can use them to create environments. Thinking about the kind of thought we are trying to develop, we can choose materials and problems to pose, things for children to think with.

One of the purposes of this sort of environment is to create common experiences from which we can bridge to the academic knowledge we want to teach. If the environment is rich enough, we will learn a lot about what children understand already by watching and listening to them. We do not have to know how the environment will work.

When we create learning environments, we begin with large collections of things and then watch to see what children do with them. We eliminate things that do not work well. We often can borrow, from museums and from other teachers, collections of materials from which to create interesting environments.

In some schools, teachers cooperate with each other in creating environments that interest them and sharing them with one another. For example, in investigating sound with a group of third graders, we brought in various instruments and devices that make sounds, drinking straws and scissors to make flutes, an oscilloscope to allow us to "see" sound, and members of the boys' choir to sing and talk about singing. We also had a device with handles on each end and wires between that could be used (we thought) to simulate the way sound waves travel. We set all of this up in a room and watched and listened.

We immediately discovered that the sound wave device didn't work at all. The children didn't even notice how the sound waves traveled. They just tried to make the device go as fast as they could. Some of the drums did not draw much attention, except that children would drum briefly as they passed by. We noted with interest that the flutes made from drinking straws that could be cut to produce ever higher sounds were engaging and generated interesting questions.

Observation and Intervention

When children are working in a learning environment, teachers are freed from directing and telling and can walk around and observe. We have to develop this ability to observe learning. At first we tend to look too fast and act too fast. This is an old habit, and getting beyond it takes time. We also tend, at first, to look at how children are behaving rather than how they are thinking.

One way to learn is to watch one child at a time and make notes about what that child is doing, trying to stay with what we see and hear without interpreting or attempting to come to any conclusions. Reading descriptions, such as those in Piaget's work, can provide a context for thinking about some of the ways children think. The most important change is to move from thinking about whether students are "getting" some idea to just noticing, by what they say and what they do, what they think and what it means to them.

After we have observed for a while, we might see places where we want to intervene. Some interventions keep children within the boundaries of a problem. Other interventions simply help a child see how to do something. Sometimes in response to learning, we share a thought or a bit of information. Sometimes an intervention is needed to help a student who is "stuck."

The first two kinds of interventions should be immediate. For example, we asked children to build houses of cards so that they could solve a problem requiring them to pay attention to center of gravity and the like. Jane was bending the cards so she no longer had to balance them against each other. The cards would stand on their own. This changed the problem, and I asked her not to do it.

Another time, we had created a measurement environment. One of the problems was to find out how many 1/4, 1/3, and 1/2 cups of uncooked rice were needed to have the same amount as 1 cup of uncooked rice. Robert obviously had no experience with using measuring cups. He wasn't paying attention to how full the cup was—sometimes filling it to the top and other times not. He did not have to figure this out. He needed to know how to use the measuring cup so he could notice the relationships between measures—which was what he did need to think about. I showed Robert the 1/4, 1/3, 1/2, and 1 cup marks and how to fill the cup to the 1 cup mark. Once he knew that, he could work on the problem.

The other two kinds of interventions require more thought and caution. When we see a child who seems to be "stuck," we have to observe long enough to get an idea about what is keeping the child from moving.

In Chapter 6, I presented a situation in which students were solving a problem called the "diabolical cube." We noticed some students beginning the task by fitting the pieces together to make a five-cube wall. They consistently did this and did not seem to understand that once one side is larger than three, they cannot build a 3 × 3 × 3 cube.

As discussed previously, Kathleen, one of the teachers, sat at the table with her own set of puzzle pieces and began constructing a five-cube wall. Then she said to herself (loudly enough so the students could hear): "Oh, no, that won't work. It's already larger than three cubes." After Kathleen did that a few times, some of the children began noticing the size of their pieces as they constructed the walls. Others did not. Kathleen's actions and comments were part of the learning context for students who were able to use them.

Discipline

The way we handle discipline and try to impose order often gets in the way of creating good learning environments in which children feel comfortable and cared for. It doesn't have to be that way. In addition to teaching math, science, and the other subjects, we are teaching children to live in a free, democratic society and to be contributing members of a community. One of our most important concerns should be in creating the conditions that support this purpose.

Imposing Consequences Versus Teaching Societal Values and Norms

Many teachers have told me that they try to discipline children by "imposing consequences." To learn from consequences, we have to be able to see the connection between our action and the consequence, we have to know another way to act, and we have to be able to make the change. This is much more complicated than simply imposing a consequence, or even allowing the consequence to happen.

Every moment in the classroom is about teaching and learning. Every encounter I have with a student is an opportunity to build a relationship and to teach the student something. Children need so much more than knowledge of the material world. They need to know everything that we know about how to be a person. Every adult has the responsibility to help any child we encounter on his or her way to adulthood, and this is the particular mission of teachers.

Principles that most adults use as a guide for our lives and that are part of most spiritual and ethical systems of thought are the principles that children need to learn. When a child hits another child, the problem is not to control the child's behavior. The educational problem is to teach the child the values and norms of adult society. The child needs to understand where he or she is wrong, make restitution, and try to act differently in the future.

Teaching children to care about one another is time well spent. When two students have a problem, such as hitting one another, I have asked both of them to tell what it was like. I've told them that I'm not concerned about trying to figure out whose fault it was because, in my experience, determining fault isn't possible, and even if it were, it wouldn't help. Students often have to be reminded about that, and they also have to be reminded to let one person finish her or his entire story before trying to tell his or her version.

These reminders were my job in the process. When each person had told what the experience was like for him or her, I posed the problem that had to be solved. Usually the problem was that we had three people who felt badly—the two of them and me. The solution to that problem would involve some mutually agreeable restitution.

In one situation, after each person had told her side, I posed the problem as, "Valerie feels sad because she was hit, and Mary feels sad because she didn't really mean to hurt Valerie like that. I feel sad because I don't like to see two great kids hurt and sad." Next I proposed that they find a solution to the bad feelings: "Sometimes it helps if we can do something to make it up to the other person. Then we can all feel better. Mary, can you think of anything you can do to help Valerie?"

When I ask that question, I receive a range of answers from, "Tell her I'm sorry" to "Pick her some flowers." Then I ask the person who was hit— Valerie, in this case—if she thinks the proposed solution will help. Most often the child says yes, and the incident ends. Sometimes it doesn't.

One hitter said she wanted to say she was sorry and the one who was hit said, "Sorry won't help." We continued to think about what might help. The child who was hit decided nothing would help, that she would just have to be sad for a while until it "leaked out."

As I participated in this process, I realized how seldom we allow children to deal with the real consequences of what they do. Most of the time, adults intervene with a punishment and the child never knows what actually happened. The simplicity of the process in the example is that the hitter got to find out what being hit was like from the point of view of the one who was hit, and the one who was hit got to find out what it was like to be provoked. Usually, at some point, the aggressor says, "I didn't mean for that to happen."

Time seems to be at such a premium in school that teachers often do not view misbehavior as an opportunity. We see it as a disturbance or a disruption that must be quelled immediately. In reacting this way, I think we miss two important opportunities:

1. Misbehavior that is generally widespread is usually symptomatic of a problem in the classroom, not in the student.
2. If we spend time helping students to develop the ability to work together and solve their own problems early in the year, we will have fewer disruptions later in the year.

The methods of "discipline" used in many classrooms do not have that effect.

Symptom Carrying

In thinking of disturbances in my classes as an opportunity to learn something about my teaching, I ask myself (even if only one student is involved) whether that person could be a symptom-carrier for the whole class. When I was young, I was the class clown, willing to get a laugh by getting in trouble to relieve the boredom of a dull lesson. The other students' comments after class indicated that they had been bored, too. In this case, I was the symptom-carrier for the class's boredom.

When one of my students creates a disturbance, I think about why this behavior is disturbing to me. Sometimes it is merely something that makes me uncomfortable because of my own personal history. Knowing that helps me not to blame the student but to make a simple request that the behavior stop for my own comfort.

As discussed in Chapter 4, Brenda, a kindergarten teacher, was having trouble with discipline. You will recall that when she tried to get the children to sit quietly and listen as she read a book to them, they would fidget and move around. In an experiment, Brenda read to the students one day while allowing them to fidget and move about the room. Afterward, she asked them about the book and was astonished to find that they had heard every word.

Brenda also realized that reading under those conditions was uncomfortable for her. She then was able to admit to the children that, although she knows they can listen while they are moving around, she has a hard time reading, so she will have to ask the children to sit quietly so she is able to read. The class seemed to understand that.

Sometimes the disruption is genuine. A student is preventing him- or herself and others from learning. I ask myself whether this is a curriculum problem. Have I created a learning environment that either is not engaging or is so narrow that some students cannot find a place in it? As Bill, a graduate student, once said, "The environment has to be rich enough that all students can get their arms around something." Only when I can truly assure myself that this is the case do I assume that the problem might be one the student brought with him or her.

If the problem is with curriculum, I have to find ways to change it. Curriculum materials and consultation with other teachers can be helpful here. Some teachers also have found that exchanging classes is helpful sometimes, with each teacher creating his or her favorite environment.

Changing Interaction

We come into social settings with a history of interactions with others. Most of the time we adapt to a new situation and a new set of people and learn new ways to interact. Some students, however, bring with them a history that makes it harder for them to respond.

Shauna, age 6, was one of those kids. When our usual process for preventing fighting didn't seem to be having a long-term effect with Shauna, I asked her to tell me how she felt. Of course, she didn't know. Most kids don't have words for feelings. I asked Shauna if she could tell me what *color* her feeling was . . . what shape . . . where it was located.

She said it was black and brown and had sharp edges and was all knotted up. She said it was "right here"—pointing to her right side just next to her belly button.

I asked her what she thought we could do to make it not so sharp or not so black. Shauna said she didn't know. She usually just "leaked it out."

We discussed the idea that she couldn't leak it on other people, and we finally agreed that when she felt that way, she could go out in front, sit on the railroad tie, and pound it until she felt better. Shauna did that a lot at first. Later she wasn't out there as much. More important, she didn't get into any more fights.

Valerie perpetually was in some sort of minor trouble. The teachers talked about this and agreed that Valerie seemed to be doing things to get attention. Although they thought her activity was a bad thing, it seemed legitimate to me. I was glad to know what the problem was. I asked Valerie to come and see me. I told her that the teachers thought she might be trying to get attention, and the way she was doing it was causing trouble for her and the people around her. I suggested that when she wanted attention, she should make an appointment with me and she could have my undivided attention for 15 minutes.

During the first month, I saw Valerie every day. We had some great conversations, but I had difficulty dropping what I was doing and being available. This probably turned out to be as good for me as it was for Valerie. After a while, the appointments became less frequent; after a couple of months, I seldom saw Valerie's name in my appointment book.

We often take problems away from children by imposing order instead of letting the order emerge so they are part of it. To live with the chaos that precedes it is difficult, and that might be why we so often do not allow children to deal with the results of their actions. For my own comfort level, it is okay to decide to impose certain order. At the same time, I have to be clear about why I am doing it and to be thoughtful about the situations in which I will let the kids work things out and those in which I will intervene.

Summary

T eaching can be a fun, exciting, growing experience. We can create conditions that help children learn to think and interact with one another in healthy, helpful ways. We have to abandon some of the ideas about teaching that were developed in the industrial revolution.

Ideas evolve. Individuals' thoughts evolve, and cultural thought evolves. We have an obligation to prepare children to contribute to the evolution of culture, as well as to benefit from the culture. We need a balance between passing on what is known and preparing children to generate new knowledge. We no longer are trying to create obedient assembly-line workers. We are trying to nurture the growth of the next generation of thoughtful, creative, caring adults.

Epilogue

I f your ideas about teaching and learning have changed as a result of having read this book, I invite you to continue to grow. I hope that these ideas continue to help you in your personal development. Above all, the message is to *watch* children. Watch them closely, and talk with them whenever you can, as Piaget did. Develop the habit of careful observation. Practice listening to children and following their interests and thoughts instead of trying to lead them to what you believe they should think or find interesting. Practice talking with children as you would a friend. Especially be aware of how often you question children, and see if you can learn to have a conversation with them instead.

From Piaget's work, we know that people have different understandings of things, and we need to try to understand a person in his or her own context. I have had the very human habit of translating what other people say and do in terms of my own frame of reference. I assume you mean what I would mean by the words you use, or I interpret your actions in terms of the meaning they would have if I were acting. I encourage you to develop another habit: Practice assuming that you do not automatically understand others. Ask them questions until you are clear what they mean by what they say or do.

This is particularly crucial in dealing with children, because they think so differently from adults.

Recall Chapter 5, where we explored how differently children understand observation of liquid. Piaget's book *The Child's Conception of the World* (1952) is filled with examples of similar differences between children's and adults' understanding of everyday things and events. He quotes a 3-year-old who says, "Tell me, Mamma, is it God who turns on the tap in the sky so that water runs through the holes in the floor of the sky?" (p. 285). You may notice the resemblance in this case between the child's view and the beliefs of ancient peoples discussed in Chapter 1.

In another case, when asked, "What is thunder?" a 9-year-old says, "It's two clouds meeting, and that makes lightning. First they touch and they hit one another, and that makes the thunder and lightning" (Piaget, 1952, p. 310). Children's views are fascinating when we learn to listen to them for how they think instead of listening for where they are wrong.

Understanding people in context matters. It also is helpful in improving relationships with adults. I have found it fun to see if I am a good enough detective to truly construct a frame of reference other than my own. I practice listening to people and thinking about what being them is like. I try to get into their heads.

Practice focusing on relationships instead of materials. Remember the exercise in which we looked at our fingers in two different ways? Whenever you look at your hands, let it remind you to focus on relationships. Try to see the connectedness rather than the differences. Practice living as if causality is circular. Look for the complexity, and beware of simple charts and simple answers, especially when thinking about human beings.

No matter how certain knowledge might seem to you, all knowledge is partial and constructed. Even physicists know that their descriptions of the physical world are about nature as we observe it, not nature as it is. If you think you know truth, I suggest that you intentionally seek out someone who disagrees with you and listen to that person's point of view until you understand how he or she can think that way. This doesn't mean you will (or even that you should) change your point of view. It means that your thinking will grow by understanding other perspectives.

One day I met with some people from the communications office of my university. My colleague and I were trying to explain what we wanted to do with some grants we had received. No matter how we explained it, we couldn't seem to make it clear. The listeners thought we were trying to introduce a new method, a new way of doing the same old things. Finally one of them understood what we were really saying. He got a shocked look on his face as he said, "Oh, you're talking about completely re-engineering teaching." Not only is that what I'm talking about, I don't think anything less will work.

If you are convinced that education must change, I invite you to become a part of creating that change. You might change the way you teach or the way you are as a parent. You might participate in trying to change schools or other places where teaching and learning take place. At the very least, you and I can change ourselves and the way we interact with children.

References

Ainsworth, M. D. S., Blehar, M. C., Waters, E., & Wall, S. (1978). *Patterns of Attachment: A Psychological Study of the Strange Situation*. Hillsdale, NJ: Erlbaum.

Ames, A. (1951). Visual Perception and the Rotating Trapezoidal Window. *Psychological Monographs* 65(7). Washington, DC: American Psychological Association.

Andrews, R., Biggs, M., & Seidel, M. (Eds.). (1996). *The Columbia World of Quotations*. New York: Columbia University Press. Retrieved July 2004 from www.bartleby.com/66/.

Atkinson, R. C., & Shiffrin, R. M. (1968). Human Memory: A Proposed System and Its Control Processes. In K. Spence and J. Spence (Eds.), *The Psychology of Learning and Motivation* (Vol. 2). New York: Academic Press.

Bateson, G. (1972). *Steps to an Ecology of Mind*. New York: Chandler.

Bateson, G. (1988). *Mind and Nature: A Necessary Unity*. New York: Macmillan.

Bateson, G. (1991). *Sacred Unity: Further Steps to an Ecology of Mind*. New York: HarperCollins.

Bateson, G., & Bateson, M. C. (1987). *Angels Fear: Toward an Epistemology of the Sacred*. New York: Macmillan.

Bateson, M. C. (1972). *Our Own Metaphor*. Washington, DC: Smithsonian Institution Press.

Beilin, H., & Pufall, P. (1992). *Piaget's Theory: Prospects and Possibilities*. Hillsdale, NJ: Lawrence Erlbaum.

Berk, L. E. (1994, November). Vygotsky's Theory: The Importance of Make-Believe Play. *Young Children*.

Beth, E., & Piaget, J. (1966). *Mathematical Epistemologies and Psychology* (W. Mays, Trans.). Dordrecht, Holland: D. Reidel.

Blinkov, S. M., & Glezer, I. I. (1968). *The Human Brain in Figures and Tables: A Quantitative Handbook*. New York: Plenum Press.

Bohlin, G. (2000). Attachment and Social Functioning: A Longitudinal Study from Infancy to Middle Childhood. *Social Development* 9(1), 24–39.

Bowlby, J. (1973). *Separation: Anxiety and Anger.* Volume 2 of *Attachment and Loss.* New York: Basic Books.

Bowlby, J. (1982). *Attachment and Loss.* Volume 1. *Attachment.* London: Hogarth Press. (Originally published in 1969.)

Boydston, J. (Ed.). (1980). *John Dewey, the Middle Works, 1899–1924* (Vol. 9: 1916). Carbondale: Southern Illinois University Press.

Briggs, J., & Peat, F. D. (1989). *Turbulent Mirror.* New York: Harper & Row.

Brown, S. L. (1995). Through the Lens of Play. *Revision 17,* 4–12.

Bruner, J. S. (1956). *Studies in Cognitive Growth.* New York: Wiley.

Bruner, J. (1973). *Beyond the Information Given.* New York: Norton.

Bruner, J. (1983). *Child's Talk.* New York: Norton.

Bruner, J. (1990). *Acts of Meaning.* Cambridge, MA: Harvard University Press.

Bruner, J., Oliver, R. H., & Greenfield, P. M. (1966). *Studies in Cognitive Growth.* New York: Wiley.

Burke, J. (1985). *The Day the Universe Changed.* Boston: Little, Brown.

Carlson, M. (1999). The Science of Mother's Day. Retrieved March 4, 2004, from http://whyfiles.org/087mother/4.html.

Cassidy, J. (2001). Truth, Lies, and Intimacy: An Attachment Perspective. *Attachment and Human Development* 3(2), 121–155.

Cherry, E. C. (1953). Some Experiments on the Recognition of Speech, with One and Two Ears. *Journal of the Acoustical Society of America, 25,* 975–979.

Cohen, J., & Stewart, I. (1994). *The Collapse of Chaos: Discovering Simplicity in a Complex World.* New York: Viking.

Cole, M., & Cole, S. (Eds.). (1979). *The Making of Mind.* Cambridge, MA: Harvard University Press.

Connell, J. P., & Goldsmith, H. H. (1982). A Structural Modeling Approach to the Study of Attachment and Strange Situation Behaviors. In R. N. Emde & R. J. Harmon (Eds.), *The Development of Attachment and Affiliative Systems* (pp. 213–243). New York: Plenum.

Cuny, H. (1965). *Ivan Pavlov: The Man and His Theories.* New York: P. E. Eriksson.

Damasio, A. (1994). *Descartes' Error: Emotion, Reason, and the Human Brain.* New York: Quill.

Damasio, A. (1999). *The Feeling of What Happens: Body and Emotion in the Making of Consciousness.* New York: Harcourt.

Damasio, A. (2003). *Looking for Spinoza: Joy, Sorrow, and the Feeling Brain.* Austin, TX: Harcourt, Inc.

Dewey, J. (1975). *Interest and Effort in Education.* Carbondale: Southern Illinois University Press. (Originally published in 1913.)

Diaz, R. M., Neal, C. J., & Amaya-Williams, M. (1992). The Social Origins of Self Regulation. In L. C. Moll (Ed.), *Vygotsky and Education: Instructional Implications and Applications of Sociohistorical Psychology* (pp. 127–154). New York: Cambridge University Press.

Doll, W. E. Jr. (1993). *A Post-Modern Perspective on Curriculum.* New York: Teachers College Press.

Drotar, D. (2002). Behavioral and Emotional Problems in Infants and Young Children: Challenges of Clinical Assessment and Intervention. *Infants and Young Children* 14(4), 1–5.

Duckworth, E. (1996). *The Having of Wonderful Ideas and Other Essays on Teaching and Learning* (2d ed.). New York: Teachers College Press.

Feeney, J. (1999). *Issues of Closeness and Distance in Dating Relationships: Effects of Sex and Attachment Style.* Thousand Oaks, CA: Sage.

Fraley, R. C. (2002). A Brief Overview of Adult Attachment Theory and Research. Retrieved February 2, 2004, from http://p032.psch.uic.edu/lab/attachment.htm.

Freud, S. (1963). *General Psychological Theory.* New York: Macmillan.

Fullan, M. G., & Stiegelbauer, S. (1991). *The New Meaning of Educational Change* (2d ed.). New York: Teachers College Press.

Garcia, R. (1992), The Structure of Knowledge and the Knowledge of Structure. In H. Berlin & P. Pufall (Eds.), *Piaget's Theory: Prospects and Possibilities.* Hillsdale, NJ: Lawrence Erlbaum.

Gladwell, M. (2002). *The Tipping Point: How Little Things Can Make a Big Difference.* Boston: Little, Brown.

Gleick, J. (1987). *Chaos: The Making of a New Science.* New York: Viking.

Goddard, K. S. (1993). Teaching Relationships/Learning Relationships. Unpublished master's thesis, Texas Christian University, Fort Worth, TX.

Goodall, J. (1995). Chimpanzees and Others at Play. *Revision, 17,* 14–20.

Goodman, G. (1998). Attachment Disorganization in Prepubertal Children with Severe Emotional Disturbance. *Bulletin of the Menninger Clinic, 62*(4), 490–525.

Greenough, W., Black, J., & Wallace, C. (1987). Experience and Brain Development. *Child Development 58,* 539–559.

Gruber, H., & Vonèche, J. (Eds.). (1995). *The Essential Piaget.* Northvale, NJ: Jason Aronson.

Harlow, H. (1958). The Nature of Love. *American Psychologist* 13, 573–685. Retrieved March 4, 2004, from http://psychclassics.yorku.ca/Harlow/love.htm.

Herndon, E. A. (1993). The Learning Community: Care and Dialogue in the Kindergarten Classroom. Unpublished master's thesis, Texas Christian University, Fort Worth, TX.

Hoffman, E. (1988). *The Right to Be Human.* New York: St. Martin's Press.

Holt, A., in Bateson, M. C. (1991). *Our Own Metaphor.* Washington, DC: Smithsonian Institution Press.

Inhelder, B., Caprona, D., & Cornu-Wells, A. (1987). *Piaget Today.* Hillsdale, NJ: Lawrence Erlbaum.

Inhelder, B., & Chipman, H. (1976). *Piaget and His School.* New York: Springer-Verlag.

Jung, C. G. (1968). *The Archetypes and the Collective Unconscious.* Princeton, NJ: Princeton University Press.

Kamii, C., & Clark, F. (2000). Young Children Reinvent Arithmetic—First Graders Dividing 62 by 5 (videotape). New York: Teachers' College Press.

Kauffman, S. (1963). *The Origins of Order.* New York: Oxford University Press.

Kauffman, S. (1995). *At Home in the Universe.* New York: Oxford University Press.

Kuhn, T. (1962). *The Structure of Scientific Revolutions.* Chicago: University of Chicago Press.

Kuhn, T. (1977). *The Essential Tension.* Chicago: University of Chicago Press.

Luria, A. R. (1979). *The Making of Mind.* Cambridge, MA: Harvard University Press.

Marti, E. (1996). Mechanisms of Internalisation and Externalisation of Knowledge in Piaget's and Vygotsky's Theories. In A. Tryphon & J. Vonèche (Eds.), *Piaget Vygotsky. The Social Genesis of Thought.* Hove, UK: Psychology Press.

Martin, K., & Reynolds, S. (1993). Veteran and Rookie Teachers: A Stereoptic Vision of Learning in Mathematics. *Journal of Teacher Education* 44(4), 245–253.

Maslow, A. (1970). *Motivation and Personality* (2d ed.). New York: Harper and Row.

Maturana, H. R, & Frenk, S. (1963). Directional Movement and Horizontal Edge Detectors in the Pigeon Retina. *Science* 142, 977–979.

Maturana, H. R., Lettvin, J. Y., McCulloch, W. S., & Pitts, W. H. (1960). Anatomy and Physiology of Vision in the Frog. *Journal of General Physiology* 43(6, Part 2), 129–175.

Maturana, H. R., & Varela, F. J. (1987). *The Tree of Knowledge. The Biological Roots of Human Understanding.* Boston: Shambhala Publications.

McCaslin, M., & Good, T. (1992, April). Compliant Cognition: The Misalliance of Management and Instructional Goals in Current School Reform. *Educational Researcher*, 4–6.

Mencken, H. L. (1949). *A Mencken Chrestomathy.* New York: A. A. Knopf.

Miller, G. A. (1956). The magical number seven, plus or minus two; some limits on our capacity for processing information. *Psychology Review* 63, 81–97.

Moll, L. C. (Ed.). (1990). *Vygotsky and Education. Instructional Implications and Applications of Sociohistorical Psychology.* New York: Cambridge University Press.

Neisser, U. (1976). *Cognition and Reality: Principles and Implications of Cognitive Psychology.* New York: Freeman.

Noddings, N. (1992). *The Challenge to Care in Schools.* New York: Teachers College Press.

Noddings, N. (2003). *Happiness and Education.* New York: Cambridge University Press.

Nowakowski, R. S. (1987). Basic Concepts of CNS Development. *Child Development* 58, 568–595.

Peat, F. D. (1987). *Synchronicity.* New York: Bantam Doubleday Dell.

Piaget, J. (1952). *The Child's Conception of the World.* London: Routledge & Kegan Paul.

Piaget, J. (1965). *The Child's Conception of Number.* New York: W. W. Norton. (Originally published in 1952.)

Piaget, J. (1976). *The Grasp of Consciousness: Action and Concept in the Young Child.* Cambridge, MA: Harvard University Press.

Piaget, J. (1977). *Piaget on Piaget* (Film). (Available from Yale University Media Design, New Haven, CT.)

Piaget, J. (1978). *Success and Understanding.* Cambridge, MA: Harvard University Press.

Piaget, J. (1987). *Possibility and Necessity* (Vol. 1). Minneapolis: University of Minnesota Press.

Piaget, J., & Garcia, R. (1989). *Psychogenesis and the History of Science.* New York: Columbia University Press.

Piaget, J., & Garcia, R. (1991). *Toward a Logic of Meanings*. Hillsdale, NJ: Erlbaum.

Prigogine, I., & Strengers, I. (1984). *Order Out of Chaos: Man's New Dialogue with Nature*. New York: Bantam.

Ross, M. E. (1995). *Sandbox Scientist*. Chicago: Chicago Review Press.

Sacks, O. (1996). *An Anthropologist on Mars*. New York: Random House.

Schulman, L. S. (1987). Knowledge and Teaching: Foundations of the New Reform. *Harvard Educational Review*, 57, 1–22.

Schultz, D. (1975). *A History of Modern Psychology*. San Diego: Academic Press.

Schwartz, P., & Ogilvy, J. (1979). *The Emergent Paradigm: Changing Patterns of Thought and Belief* (VALS Report No. 7). Menlo Park, CA: Values and Lifestyles Program.

Sergiovanni, T. J., & Duggan, B. (1990). Moral Authority: A Blueprint for Leading Tomorrow's Schools. In T. J. Sergiovanni & J. E. Moore (Eds.), *Target 2000—A Compact for Excellence in Texas Schools* (pp. 21–30). Trinity University, San Antonio, TX: 1990 Yearbook of the Texas Association for Supervision and Curriculum Development.

Siegel, D. (1999). *The Developing Mind: How Relationships and the Brain Interact to Shape Who We Are*. New York: The Guilford Press.

Skinner, B. F. (1974). *About Behaviorism*. New York: Vintage Books.

Taylor, S. E. (2002). *The Tending Instinct*. New York: Times Books.

Tolman, E. C. (1932). *Purposive Behavior in Animals and Men*. New York: Century.

Tryphon, A., & Vonèche, J. (Eds.). (1996). *Piaget–Vygotsky. The Social Genesis of Thought*. Hove, UK: Psychology Press.

U.S. Public Health Service. (2000). *Report of the Surgeon General's Conference on Children's Mental Health: A National Action Agenda*. Washington, D.C.: Department of Health and Human Services.

Vygotsky, L. (1978). *Mind in Society*. Cambridge, MA: Harvard University Press.

Vygotsky, L. (1986). *Thought and Language*. Cambridge, MA: MIT Press.

Waldrop, M. M. (1992). *Complexity: The Emerging Science at the Edge of Order and Chaos*. New York: Simon & Schuster.

Watzlavick, P., Weakland, J., & Fisch, R. (1974). *Change: Principles of Problem Formation and Problem Resolution*. New York: W. W. Norton.

Wertsch, J. V. (1996). The Role of Abstract Rationality in Vygotsky's Image of Mind. In A. Tryphon & J. Vonèche (Eds.), *Piaget–Vygotsky. The Social Genesis of Thought*. Hove, UK: Psychology Press.

WGBH Interactive Media. (1998). Retrieved May 2004 from http://interactive.wgbh.org/.

Wheatley, M. (1996, November). *The New Science of Leadership: An Interview with Margaret Wheatley*. In S. London (Host) [Radio program]. San Luis Obispo, CA: KCBX.

Whyte, L. L. (1951). *Aspects of Form*. London: Lund, Humphries.

Whyte, L. L. (1955). *Accent on Form*. London: Routledge & Paul.

Whyte, L. L. (1978). *The Unconscious before Freud*. London: Julian Friedmann.

Zajonc, A. (1993). *Catching the Light*. New York: Oxford University Press.

Index